THE

CHURCH OF THE REDEEMER,

AS DEVELOPED WITHIN THE

GENERAL SYNOD

OF THE

LUTHERAN CHURCH IN AMERICA.

With a Historic Outline from the Apostolic Age.

TO WHICH IS APPENDED

A PLAN FOR RESTORING APOSTOLIC UNION BETWEEN ALL ORTHODOX DENOMINATIONS.

BY

S. S. SCHMUCKER, D.D.

EMERITUS PROFESSOR OF THEOLOGY IN THE THEOLOGICAL SEMINARY, GETTYSBURG.

SECOND EDITION.

"There is one Lord, one faith, one baptism, one God and Father of all."—EP. iv. 5.

"Multum refert ad retinendum ecclesiarum pacem, inter ea quæ jure divino præcepta sunt, et quæ non sunt, accuraté distinguere." — GROTIUS, *de Imperio summarum Potestatum circa sacra; cap. II.*

BALTIMORE:
T. NEWTON KURTZ.
PHILADELPHIA: E. W. MILLER.
GETTYSBURG: A. D. BUEHLER.
1868.

J. FAGAN & SON,
STEREOTYPERS, PHILAD'A.

PREFACE.

THE origin of this small volume was somewhat peculiar. It has several times happened, that the appointed speakers of the *Historical Society of the Evangelical Lutheran Church* in the United States, whose meetings coincide with those of the General Synod, have failed to meet their appointments. This was naturally unpleasant to the Society, as well as mortifying to the writer as its present president. To prevent a similar disappointment, he resolved, several months before the late meeting of the General Synod at Fort Wayne, to prepare a Lecture to be delivered as a volunteer exercise, in case the appointee should again fail. As to a suitable subject for such exercise, the frequent late attacks on the General Synod did not permit him to hesitate. An ardent friend of this General Union of the Synods from its incipiency, he was willing to step forward in its defence, and having been present as a visitor at Baltimore in 1819, when the formation of such a body was first the subject of synodical discussion, and at Hagerstown in 1820, when the constitution was discussed and adopted; present as a member of the body in 1823, and either as a member or visitor at every meeting held since, the writer may, without vanity or presumption, profess to be acquainted with its design, history and spirit, and may ask a hearing in its behalf. Fortunately, the appointed reader, the Rev. Dr. Harkey, faithfully performed his duty, and our lecture was not offered.

Returning from Fort Wayne, the document was read on the way, in a circle of our most able and influential brethren, who strongly urged its publication, (with an historical part prefixed, and a few other additions,) as well calculated for circulation among both the laity and ministers of our church, and not without interest to the general reader. With this wish we have endeavored to comply, and now present the work to the public, and commend it to the blessing of that divine Redeemer, whose cause it is designed to vindicate.

S. S. SCHMUCKER.

GETTYSBURG, *Dec.* 25, 1866.

NOTICES OF THE PRESS.

From the Lutheran Observer.

DR. SCHMUCKER'S NEW WORK — THE CHURCH OF THE REDEEMER. — This work is not only a clear and logical history of Evangelical Lutheranism, as developed in this country, under the auspices of the General Synod, but a philosophical conspectus of her present doctrinal position and ecclesiastical polity. The work is timely, and characterized by the author's usual perspicuity of thought, logical arrangement, and masterly disposition of the controversial topics under discussion. His vindication of Evangelical Lutheranism, as held by the General Synod, and founded upon the Augsburg Confession, is demonstrative and triumphant. After reading this book, one feels a commendable pride in being a General Synod Lutheran, and can smile, in conscious repose, at the flippant but impotent thrusts at the soundness of our Lutheranism. This book ought to find a welcome in every Lutheran family.

From the American Lutheran.

THE CHURCH OF REDEEMER. By Dr. SCHMUCKER. — We are gratified to learn that this book meets with a ready and rapid sale. The first edition is already exhausted, we believe, in less than two months after its appearance. The second edition will be issued in two or three weeks. This is something unprecedented in the history of Lutheran publications in this country.

This volume contains the latest and most matured views of Dr. Schmucker on those questions that now agitate the church, and every one who wishes to make himself acquainted with the church question as viewed from the American Lutheran standpoint, should procure a copy. It is just the book that is needed to put into the hands of our ministers and people at this time, and therefore we hail its appearance and rapid sale with heartfelt joy. We predict that it will have a wide circulation, not only in our own church, but also in other christian denominations.

From the American Presbyterian.

THE CHURCH OF THE REDEEMER. By Dr. SCHMUCKER. — This is a thorough historic vindication of the character and spirit of the General Synod (the evangelical and liberal branch), of the Lutheran church in this country, and derives especial interest from the struggles and divisions now taking place in that ancient Church. One of the aims of this General Synod is stated to be the promotion of union among all Evangelical denominations, into which our author enters with zeal. Already in 1838 Prof. Schmucker had published a circular containing a detailed plan for the Confederation of all these churches, which was widely approved and signed by prominent men in each of the churches, which plan is published in an Appendix at the close of the book. There is a great deal of valuable information contained in the volume which is made accessible by a full index.

From the Methodist Home Journal.

This contribution of the learned and evangelical Dr. Schmucker will be hailed with sincere pleasure, not only by the different Lutheran Synods in this country, of the American, German, Swedish and Norwegian nationalities, to whom it is especially dedicated, but by the "Church of God in general," as a valuable and practical exposition of the primitive apostolical spirit; an epitome of Church history; and one of the most sensible and urgent overtures for Christian union we have ever met with. We could wish for space in these columns to spread before our readers the grave considerations offered, showing the possibility and importance of a mighty consolidation of the energies of Protestantism for the formation and maintenance of Christian sentiment, and the promotion of truth and righteousness throughout the world. This volume contains but little that we cannot heartily commend.

DEDICATION.

TO the different Evangelical Lutheran Synods in the United States, of all nationalities, the American, the German, the Swedish and the Norwegian, and especially those connected with the General Synod, this work is fraternally dedicated by the author.

Christian Brethren,—the original design of the General Synod of our church, in this country, was to effect a fraternal union or confederation, of limited and chiefly advisory powers, between all the Lutheran Synods then existing in our country. This object was also happily effected at the organization of that body in 1820, in regard to all those synods, except that of Ohio, which had not yet completed its connection with us in 1823. In that year the Pennsylvania Synod, after having attended a single meeting, withdrew from the union, not on account of any dissatisfaction with its principles, (for they expressly affirmed the contrary,) but because their congregations had listened to the misrepresentations of ignorance and prejudice, which were caught up and circulated in their congregations by political demagogues, for selfish purposes. The charges, forsooth, were, that the General Synod, the Bible Societies, Tract Societies and Theological Seminaries, were all parts of a secret scheme to unite Church and State, and to introduce into our church in this country religious coercion, like that of the Fatherland. Thirty years afterwards, the Pennsylvania Synod again united with the General Synod.

All the different synods of other nationalities, now amongst us, are of more recent origin in our country. During the half century of the General Synod's existence, a portion of the churches in Europe have passed from one extreme of confessional indifference to the other of rigid symbolism.

The General Synod also has, during the same period, experienced some change in the same direction, but in a far more moderate degree, still adhering, in the main, to the fundamental principles of her union, and the liberty of difference on topics of nonessential moment. The Scandinavians and Germans, of more recent immigration, naturally sympathize with the symbolic status of their native lands, and therefore find themselves, in some measure, at variance with our General Synod. Some of them have already felt the influence of our free institutions, and a quarter of a century will teach them fully to appreciate the apostolic liberty of our country, and to feel the obligation it imposes on them. Then, or even sooner, the great body of them will, if we mistake not, occupy the apostolic ground of our General Synod. We therefore cordially invite all, who do not approve the status of the General Synod, to accompany us through the pages of this work, in which the principles in question are examined and traced to their original sources. Some of the historical portions may be passed over lightly by the learned, as they were added for the benefit of the popular reader.

To those, therefore, who are friends of the rigid symbolic system of the post-Lutheran era of the Reformation, as practised for two centuries in our church in Germany, we would say, in the premises, that our standpoint differs materially from theirs.

Our rigidly symbolic friends regard obedience

to extended and minute human confessions as an undoubted duty; whilst we suppose it unscriptural, yea, anti-scriptural and sinful. They speak much about fidelity to human creeds or symbols, whilst we regard fidelity to the Bible, to God's own word, as not only entirely and invariably paramount, but also as a duty, claiming far more constant and prayerful attention.

In common with the friends of the General Synod, we can find no explicit authority in God's word, for any human symbols or confessions at all, as tests, to admit or exclude men from the Church of the Redeemer; the Scriptures alone being supposed to be sufficient for this purpose.* Even by inferential reasoning, we can justify only a short creed, containing those leading doctrines of the Gospel, which experience proves to be necessary to co-operation among true believers, and not all that is demanded by narrow-minded bigots.

* *Rev.* xxii. 18, 19: "For I testify unto every man that heareth the words of the prophecy of this book, if any man shall add unto these things, God shall add unto him the plagues that are written in this book," &c. *Deut.* iv. 2: "Ye shall not add to the word which I command you, neither shall ye diminish aught from it, that ye may keep the commandments of the Lord your God, which I command you."

Such is the Augsburg Confession, which we highly approve as received by the General Synod. Under virtually such regulations the primitive church enjoyed her highest prosperity and most rapid extension—her golden age—during the ante-Nicene period. In assuming her present liberal standpoint, rejecting as tests all the former symbolic books, except the Augsburg Confession, and conceding binding authority to that, only so far as the fundamental doctrines of the Scriptures are concerned,—

The General Synod undeniably returns, in substance, to the practice of the primitive ages of the Christian Church.

She regards herself as having accomplished a vast improvement in the organic structure of the church, and a most important step towards that union among his disciples, for which the Saviour poured forth his sacerdotal prayer.

All who agree in the cardinal doctrines of the New Testament can be received into the churches of the General Synod; whilst few, indeed, could be admitted into the symbolic churches, if accordance with the professed extensive symbols were consistently exacted.

Before any rigid symbolist, therefore, objects to the positions of this volume, he ought earnestly to inquire whether he can find any authority in Scripture for such a radical departure from the practice of the apostolic and primitive ages, as is that of the rigid symbolic system. That innovation is at variance with the principles and practice of the Church of Christ for 1500 years, as well as opposed to the teachings of our illustrious reformer, Luther, himself. Nor was it introduced until thirty-four years after his departure to the church triumphant in heaven.

If, therefore, the Reformation by Luther is justly applauded, because it was a return from the corruptions of Rome to the purity of the Gospel, then, also, is the standpoint of the General Synod entitled to similar approbation; because it consists in a still further approximation to the apostolic status of Christianity, and in the rejection of that system of symbolic servitude imposed on the church after Luther's death, which though not theoretically, yet practically robbed the believer of his liberty of thought and *exclusive* obligation to the word of God. The symbolist has no right to take it for granted that the successors of Luther were authorized to make this radical innovation on the principles of the Reformation, as conducted by Luther himself, with the Bible alone as his guide. Like Luther, he should feel himself a free agent, placed under the responsibility of the inspired word of God as the supreme law of the universe, higher far than any human symbols or human legislation. Like Luther, he should examine the infallible Word, in which are described the doctrines, the organization, and worship enjoined by the Saviour and his apostles. He should compare the church as he now finds it, with the principles of the inspired model, and whatever additions have been made, adverse to that word, he should condemn as Luther did, and use his utmost endeavors to bring back the church to her primitive purity and legitimate development. He should permit no one, neither the Pope nor Luther, nor Calvin, nor Wesley, to stand between him and the inspired Word. There are, indeed, few periods in the world's history, in which the Hand divine, that rules the world, has brought about so favorable a combination of circumstances as that which bestowed such wonderful success on the labors of Luther, and the want of which led Huss to the stake. Yet is it the duty of every man, within the sphere of his own influence, be that great or small, to work by Luther's rule, the infallible word of God; and labor to bring himself, the church and the world into accord with its dictates, leaving the result with Providence.

As the symbolist can find no scriptural authority for rigid symbolic requisitions, he must return with the General Synod to the Bible, as the sole rule of faith and practice, and by this standard alone do the positions of this volume claim to be judged. The eternal destiny of the symbolist himself will be finally decided, not by his fidelity to human creeds, but according to the faithfulness with which he adhered to that only infallible guide given us by God, in opposition to all conflicting human authority. There is a world-wide difference between fidelity to God's word and fidelity to uninspired creeds. *The former is always right; the latter often wrong.*

How strange and mournful is it, that good men, at this late day, and with the experience of a thousand years before them, can still find it in their hearts to disturb the peace of the church of Christ, and rend its unity, on account of a few nonessential, abstract points of difference, such as the mode of the Saviour's presence in the eucharist; which the church, after a thousand years of contention, has failed to settle, and which, in the judgment of impartial men, is not decided in Scripture! Ought not the true disciples of the Lord inquire, whether they can justify this course at the bar of their God? Ought not the radical studies of our learned German brethren lead them back, in this free country, to this first principle — this apostolic practice?

The Moravian church adopts the Augsburg Confession, as well as we do, and yet has never had any contention on this subject, because she admits diversity of views, yea, even makes special provision for the communion of Lutheran and Reformed church-members with her by her so-called tropes.

The Presbyterian, the Episcopal, and the Methodist churches have language embodied in their creeds, from which the doctrine of the real presence could easily be deduced; and yet they have had no contention on this subject, because they also allow difference of opinion in regard to it.

Oh, when will our Lutheran brethren cease to embitter each other's life and retard the work of their common Saviour by their mutual criminations and contentions. When will they be willing to dwell in unison together, and help to bear each other's burdens, although they cannot think alike on all minor subjects. The early Christians themselves, as *Origen* informs us, held different views on several topics, and yet did not sever their ecclesiastical relations, nor disturb the peace of the church. The tendency of the rigid, symbolic system is obviously to warp our judgment on the relative importance of different truths, and to habituate the mind to an over-estimate of minor shades of doctrine. Else how account for the fact, that some writers of this class have been so blind, as unblushingly to announce the startling position, that every doctrine of the Augsburg Confession (if not of all the other symbols also) is fundamental? Did not the blessed

Saviour himself denounce certain individuals, who, whilst they were attentive to matters of less moment, neglected the "*weightier* matters of the law, judgment, mercy and faith"? Now, if some of the divine injunctions or truths are "more weighty," others must be less; and the position, that all the teachings or doctrines of the Augsburg Confession, or of other symbols, are of equal importance, is not only a psychological absurdity, but also contrary to the instructions of the Saviour himself.

As to myself, should this be my last utterance touching this subject, I cheerfully testify that I feel happy in looking back on nearly fifty years of my life spent, not in building up the walls of sectarianism, but in laboring to promote the kingdom of Christ in the Lutheran Church, on the most Catholic or liberal principles,—building it up with constant recognition of the other evangelical denominations. I rejoice that my life and action have been in consonance with the Saviour's prayer: "Holy Father, keep through thine own name, those whom thou hast given me, that they may be one as we are."—"Neither pray I for these alone, (not for the apostolic twelve alone, nor for the then existing body of believers alone;) but for them also who shall believe in me through their word, that they may *all* be one, as Thou, Father, art in me and I in thee; that they also may be one in us, *that the world may believe that*

Thou hast sent me." And I confidentially anticipate the Master's approbation on my labors, in behalf of the object of his prayer, at the final day, however feeble they may have been. Absolute external union of denominations is not necessary to Christian union; but the Christianity of conflicting sects, of Paul, of Apollos, or of Cephas, of Luther, of Zwingli and Calvin, is certainly not the Christianity of the New Testament. Nothing will fully effect the desired apostolic unity short of such a voluntary stated union or intercourse between the different evangelical denominations or parts of the Church of Christ, as will imply and produce unity of spirit and mutual good will,—a union formed and sustained, not by amalgamation into one body, but by reciprocal ministerial recognition, by occasional sacramental communion, by regulations of non-interference in missionary operations, and by active co-operation in associations for objects of common interest, such as Bible Societies, and, to some extent, Tract Societies, Sunday School Unions, &c. This will involve and sustain the unity indicated by the Master; and these are the principles fostered by the ecclesiastical organism of our noble, apostolic *General Synod of the Evangelical Lutheran Church in this country.* These principles, if sincerely embraced, both in their positive and negative side,—both as to the cardinal doctrines the belief of which is required, and the nonessentials in regard to which liberty of difference is to be cordially and peaceably conceded,—will speedily unite into one confederation or advisory body all our different synods in the land. Happy will be the day when our synods of all nationalities, yet standing aloof from us, shall have learned to distinguish between the fundamentals of God's word, as set forth in the Augsburg Confession, and the nonfundamentals contained in this and in the other confessional books; and when grace shall have made them willing, whilst holding fast to the former, to co-operate harmoniously with those brethren who, though agreeing with them in these, yet differ from them in some points of minor importance. Then may we hope to see all our synods, the American, the German, the Swedish and Norwegian, harmoniously "working together for the furtherance of the Gospel" of Jesus Christ, and harmoniously associated in the General Synod; each District Synod retaining the immediate control of all its own affairs, and yet preventing interference, harmonizing their plans, and promoting efficiency in action by unity of counsel through the *General Synod. Utinam Deus faxit!*

S. S. SCHMUCKER.

TABLE OF CONTENTS.

THE CHURCH OF THE REDEEMER.

CHAPTER I.

The Church of God in General.

THE subject to which the attention of the reader is invited, is the Church of the Redeemer, one of the most important topics that can engage the attention of men or angels. In the oracles of God, this Church is designated by the most endearing names, and interesting tropes. She is termed the *Zion* of the Holy One of Israel,—the *heritage* of God,—the *Holy Hill*, the *loved of God*. We are told that *God will place salvation in her*, and will *reign in her*, that *Christ is her king*, and that God commands the *blessing* there, *even life for evermore*.

When perusing these glowing descriptions, we must not forget, that both in the Greek and Hebrew

Scriptures,* the words rendered church, signify a collection of *persons and not of things or places.* We must withdraw our attention from the visible structure made by men's hands, from the brick and mortar of the material edifice, in which the worship of God is conducted. The church or temple of the Lord consists of the redeemed souls, purchased by the blood of Christ, and sanctified by the Holy Spirit dwelling in them. Paul characterizes the Corinthian believers as the temple of God; and the true or invisible church of Christ, in general, may be defined to be the *collective body of all true believers on earth,* in whom the Holy Spirit has his dwelling or habitation.†

* קָהָל in O. Test., and ἡ ἐκκλησία in N. Test., Genesis xxxv. 11, and xvi. 18, &c.

† The *Augsburg Confession,* Article VII., thus defines the church: "Ecclesia est congregatio sanctorum, in qua evangelium recte docetur, et recte administrantur sacramenta." "The church is the congregation of saints, in which the gospel is correctly taught, and the sacraments are properly administered."

The *Helvetic Confession,* c. 17: "Ecclesia i.e. e mundo evocatus et collectus cœtus fidelium." "The church is the assembly of the faithful, who have been called and collected from the world."

The *Anglican Confession,* or 39 Art. of the Church of England, Art. XIX.: "The visible Church of Christ is a congregation of faithful men, in the which the pure word of God is preached, and the sacraments be duly administered

The conception of the Church of *God* in this spiritual acceptation, is a glorious one! It is an association of rational and immortal beings, united together for the purpose of cultivating proper feelings, as well as resolutions of absolute, eternal obedience to the great Author of the Universe, the Creator of our spirits, the Governor of all worlds.

Church of the *Redeemer!* — How much more glorious still is the conception! A society of immortal, intelligent, and moral agents, who by transgression had fallen from God, who were justly condemned to everlasting misery on account of their manifold transgressions, and were unable to deliver themselves. A society whom God himself, the offended judge, compassionated, and for whom he sent his only Son, to assume our nature, to yield a perfect obedience to the law in our stead, and then to lay down his life a ransom, an atonement for the sins of a rebel world.

This noble institution embraces all the faithful

according to Christ's ordinance, in all those things, that of necessity are requisite to the same."

The *Westminster Confession*, Chap. XXV. ii.: "The visible church, which is also catholic or universal under the gospel, (not confined to one nation as before under the law,) consists of all those throughout the world, that profess the true religion, together with their children; and is the kingdom of the Lord Jesus Christ, the house and family of God, out of which there is no ordinary possibility of salvation."

followers of the Redeemer, of all ages and countries, of all climates and all complexions. The burning Hindoo and the freezing Esquimaux, belong to it, as also the purest white of the temperate zone of Europe and America, and the deepest jet of the African beneath the torrid sun, the converted Jew, and the Christianized Pagan. All, all are comprehended in this glorious Church of the Redeemer, and belong to the goodly fellowship of the prophets, to the noble army of martyrs, and to the General Assembly of the first-born, whose names are written in heaven.

How sublime an exhibition of the divine goodness and mercy is embodied in this church! How deserving of our highest gratitude and love! How infinitely important is it, that our fallen, guilty, but divinely redeemed race, should accept these proffered everlasting blessings, and be saved from the endless torments of the accursed!

Of this divine society, the church, we propose in the following pages to discuss the nature and characteristics, the history and the development. To the consideration of this interesting and momentous subject, we invite the reader's prayerful attention. And may the Holy Spirit, whom the Saviour promised to send, take possession of our hearts, and direct our thoughts, so that nothing may fall from our pen unworthy of the theme, so that all our representations may tend to persuade some poor lost sinners to take refuge from the storms of divine displeasure in this ark of safety, the Church of the Redeemer.

Yes, the Church of Christ on earth was designed as an association, not of careless, indifferent sinners, but of those who are laboring to work out their salvation with fear and trembling, in the strength of him who works in them both to will and to do. Nor should any be admitted into it, except such as have renounced the world and fully resolved to cast in their lot with the peculiar people of God, who are zealous of good works, together with their households (όιχιαις) their children. No congregation of professed Christians is worthy to be styled a Church of Christ which is not auxiliary to the work of salvation, which does not afford its members both encouragement and constant assistance in accomplishing the great end of their being, to glorify God and save their souls. This is the practical judgment even of the unconverted.

How often do we hear pastors of different denominations, whose church-members are immersed in worldliness and vanity, exhibiting merely the form of godliness without its power, and presenting none of that light of good works, which would lead others to glorify God, complain that their *serious* members are prone to leave them for other churches. It may be well for such to inquire into the cause of this phenomenon. We doubt not it will be found, that though secular calculations and secular profit frequently exert a potential influence, yet generally the cause will be found in the consciousness of the seceding members, that they will find greater inducements to a religious life, and facilities for it in the adopted church, than in their own. Instead of aiming to prevent the evil, by inculcating, especially on the young, an increase of denominational spirit, would it not be better for these pastors to pray and labor for an increase of active piety in their church, and offer more encouragement, and greater facilities, to inquiring souls in seeking and finding the Lord.

Experience, we doubt not, would vindicate this advice. For even the children of this world intend to secure their salvation at some future day, before death removes them from the land of probation. Hence, even they prefer to frequent a church which offers these facilities and encouragements, although they do not design to improve them at present. Nothing on earth can form so strong a bond of attachment in the Christian's heart toward any church, as the fact that there he was first arrested in his career of sin and indifference, and there found the Saviour. Nor can this feeling be pronounced unreasonable or wrong; for what will it profit a man if he gain the whole world and lose his own soul, or what can a man give in exchange for his soul?

CHAPTER II.

Essential Features of Christian Worship.

HAT then are the *essential features* of this heaven-descended institution, this school of salvation, this nursery for the celestial world, as seen on the pages of the New Testament?

The cardinal command of our Lord to his disciples was, to go and *preach the gospel*, the glad tidings of salvation, to every creature.

I. *Preaching* is therefore one of the principal ordinances of God's house, and the chief means by which the kingdom of Christ is to be promoted on earth. Indeed *all the appointed means are resolvable into* TRUTH, *preached either orally, symbolically, or in writing*. The burden of this preaching, the cardinal doctrines to be proclaimed, are: 1. That all men are by nature and practice sinners, rebels against the righteous government of God, and unable by their own strength either to convert or save themselves. 2. That they are under the righteous displeasure of God, and condemnation of his law. 3. That God in mercy has compassionated their lost and undone condition, and so loved the world as to give his only-begotten Son, that whosoever believeth in him should not perish, but have everlasting life. 4. That all who give heed to this proclamation of divine love and mercy, who have learned to see and repent of their sins, and resolved to renounce them, are to unite in an association for mutual edification and encouragement in the ways of God.

II. To this association or church is the duty entrusted, of having the gospel of the kingdom, the gracious purposes and plans of God, statedly expounded to themselves, and of laboring, in conjunction with others, to spread the knowledge of God's word over the entire globe.

III. To this church also is entrusted the administration of the holy sacraments, baptism, and the Lord's supper; by which the church is distinguished from the world, and by which those spiritual benefits, indicated by these sacraments, are offered to all, and conferred on every worthy recipient.

IV. The essentials of the church-service are preaching, prayer, singing, the sacraments, together with church government and discipline, the general nature of which is fixed in Scripture; but the circumstances of which are left to experience of every age, in their adaptation to the peculiar condition of the church, in her progressive development.

This blessed institution has experienced various vicissitudes, both prosperous and adverse in different ages and countries, where it has been established, until the time of the glorious Reformation. Then the chains were broken which bound the church in all the empires and kingdoms of Europe, in one external organization, to the papal throne at Rome; and the different nations obtained liberty to organize the church within their bounds, according to their own convictions of Scriptural injunction. Some knowledge of this antecedent history of the whole church is necessary to an enlightened appreciation of the development of any particular part of it; as a knowledge of the general geography of the earth, its form, dimensions, divisions, &c., is necessary to an intelligent and minute study of any particular country.

CHAPTER III.

Historical Sketch.

THE CHRISTIAN CHURCH DURING THE FIRST FOUR CENTURIES.

BOUT fifteen hundred years had passed away, from the time when the Son of God descended from heaven to redeem our fallen race, till the ever memorable Reformation of the church from papal corruptions by the Protestant Reformers. Various vicissitudes attended the church during this period. In the beginning the apostles went from one country to another, preaching the unsearchable riches of Christ; and the Christian doctrines, wherever faithfully presented and willingly received, proved themselves effectual, by the Spirit's aid, to satisfy all the necessities of our fallen nature.

Everywhere, but first in cities and towns, where an audience could most easily be collected, and where the superior intelligence of the hearers qualified them better to appreciate the gospel, their efforts were crowned with signal success. Sinners were awakened and converted, and clusters of converts were organized into churches, which became points of attraction and admiration to surrounding heathen. During the first four centuries, the church preserved comparative purity. Although errorists arose,* the great body of believers remained faithful to the truth as it is in Jesus, and rejoiced to behold continued additions to the church, of "such as were saved" from the dominion and the curse of sin. The persecuting rage of Pagan priests and rulers was for centuries expended in vain. Tortures the most inhuman were inflicted on Christians, in order to induce them to recant and abandon their profession. "The inhuman rulers commanded them to be scourged with whips, to be scorched by applying heated brazen plates to the most tender parts of the body. To prepare them for the renewal of such barbarous treatment, they were remanded to prison, and again brought forth, some to a repetition of similar cruelties, others to die under the hands of their persecutors. Various were the ways in which the martyrs were called to suffer death: some were

* The principal errors and heresies which appeared in this period were, Judaizing tendencies, different forms of Gnosticism, Montanism, Manichæism, Arianism, &c.

thrown to wild beasts, others roasted in an iron chair, and many were beheaded." But the blood of martyrs proved to be the seed of the church. The few fishermen and tentmakers, sustained by their invisible but divine Master, fought their way against the pride of power, the pomp of opulence, and the sensuality of lust, until the banners of Christianity, which were first unfurled in the valleys of Judea, were waving in triumph over the palace of the Cæsars; and Rome, the mistress of the world, was compelled to do homage to the crucified Nazarene.

UNION OF CHURCH AND STATE UNDER CONSTANTINE.

But the gradual union of Church and State under Constantine the Great and his successors, in the fourth century, ultimately exerted a deleterious influence. The grant of fixed salaries to ministers, and various other immunities, such as exemption from the performance of military and also of some civil duties, and the legal sanction of numerous bequests to the church, tended eventually to secularize the ministers and divert their attention from the spiritual duties of their holy calling. It favored the introduction of more ostentatious forms and ceremonies into the public worship, and diverted both ministers and people from their great vocation, to labor for the conversion of the world. Eventually the bishops were invested with civil and criminal jurisdiction over the priests, and in specific cases over others also, and thus civil and ecclesiastical governments were commingled to the detriment of both.

RISE OF PAPACY.

The establishment of popery in the seventh century completed the subjection of the church to corrupt and secularizing influences. When in A. D. 606, the tyrannical Greek emperor Phocas, in order to secure the favor of Boniface the III., bishop of Rome, was induced to acknowledge him as the head of the universal church on earth, even over the bishop of his own capital, Constantinople: and when in A. D. 794, at the downfall of the kingdom of the Lombards, and of the Exarchate of Ravenna, the latter territory was granted by Pepin, king of France, to the Roman See, and the pope was thus also made a temporal prince; the death-blow was given to spirituality in the Romish church. The popes, cardinals, and bishops were still more inflated by their civil elevation, and finally lost the spirit of Him, who said, "My kingdom is not of this world." Vital godliness was in a great measure banished from the church, and though God had at all times a seed to serve him, it is appalling to contemplate the corruption pervading the visible head and members of the church, and their total forgetfulness of the grand object of their sacred vocation.

The popes themselves were not unfrequently infidels, even denying the immortality of the soul, and their courts the seats of the most debasing licentiousness and debauchery. The pretended celibacy of the priests, which, after having for several centuries been introduced in different places, was universally enforced by pope Gregory VII., celebrated for his licentious intrigues with princess Matilda, in the eleventh century, produced the most disastrous consequences. According to the testimony of Romish authors themselves, such as Clemangis, George Cassander, St. Ligori, and the late Cardinal de Ricci, the most appalling scenes of corruption and licentiousness characterized not only the nunneries and monasteries, but also the private priests, bishops, and popes.* Even entire councils have testified to the same fact, such as the council of Moguntia, A.D. 800, the council Enhamense, A.D. 1009, and others of later date. In short, so loud and urgent was the call for a reformation, even by many among the Romanists them-

* For extensive particulars and authorities to prove this general corruption, in modern as well as ancient nunneries and priests, in America as well as in Europe, we refer the reader to our Discourse on the Reformation, ed. 5th, pp. 42 to 66, and passim; and to other authors there named.

selves, that the council of Constance, corrupt as it was, declared, A.D. 1414–18, that a reformation was needed *both in the head and members of their church!* The ignorance not only of the people, but also of the higher clergy and bishops themselves, was, even shortly before the Reformation, almost incredible. The monks attributed all heresies to the Greek and Hebrew languages, especially to the former. "The New Testament," said one of them, "is a book full of serpents and thorns." "GREEK," continued he, "is a *modern* language, but *recently invented*, and against which we must be upon our guard. As to *Hebrew*, my dear brethren, it is certain that whosoever studies *that*, immediately becomes a *Jew*."

4

CHAPTER IV.

Reformation of the Sixteenth Century.

HILST the Roman pontiff Leo X. slumbered in imaginary security at the head of the church, and saw nothing throughout the vast extent of his dominions but tranquillity and submission,* whilst the friends of genuine religion almost despaired of seeing the much longed-for reformation, an obscure and inconsiderable monk arose, on a sudden, in the year 1517, and laid the foundation of this long-expected change, by opposing himself alone, with undaunted resolution, to the torrent of papal ambition and despotism. This remarkable man was *Martin Luther*, a native of Eisleben, in Saxony, a monk of the Augustinian Eremites, and at the same time professor of theology in the University of Wittenberg, established a few years before by Frederic the Wise. "That Luther was possessed of extraordinary talents, uncommon genius, a copious memory, astonishing industry and

* See Dr. Mosheim's History in loc., McLean's version.

perseverance, superior eloquence, a greatness of soul that rose above all human weaknesses, and consummate erudition for the age in which he lived, even those among his enemies who possess some candor, do not deny." * Sustained by the hand of Providence, and aided by a numerous band of worthy coadjutors, he was enabled to carry on this glorious work, until the power of popery was broken in a large part of Europe, and the well-known Reformation was established by law.

We may premise that this wonderful revolution was not of a political character. It was not designed to give birth to a new nation, but to a new organization of the intellectual and religious energies and pursuits of the civilized world. It was regenerative of that which had been lost or dead in the interests and pursuits of men, and conservative of that which was true and good, and had thus far survived amid the mass of papal corruption. Of this grand revolution, this glorious work of reform, the celebrated historian, Dr. D'Aubigne, thus speaks:

"It is in Germany especially, that we shall see and describe the history of the Reformation. It is there we find its primitive type,—it is there that it offers the fullest development of its organization. It is there that it bears above all the marks of a revolution, not confined to one or more nations; but on the

* Murdock's Mosheim, vol. iii. p. 19.

contrary affecting the world at large. The German Reformation is the true and fundamental Reformation. It is the great planet, and the rest revolve in wider or narrower circles around it, like satellites drawn after it by its movement," etc.

The corruptions of Romanism from which the Reformation delivered those countries that embraced it, consisted in a vast amount of moral pollution, sanctioned in great measure by the superstitious rites and corrupt doctrines of the church, which encouraged every form of vice, by providing easy absolution for its perpetration. The great and constant effort of Luther was to expose the corruptions of the priesthood and church, and to restore the primitive purity of scriptural truth or doctrine.

What gave to Luther such extraordinary control over the populace in his discourses in the earlier stage of the Reformation, and such unusual success in his efforts at reform, was the fact that he was simultaneously the *subject and the agent* of the Reformation. God was at the same time reforming him, and using him to reform the church. He had been sincere in his early belief of the doctrines of popery; but was an unconverted man. Every ray of light which taught him to see one doctrinal error after another, also taught him to perceive the depravity of his own heart, filled his soul with religious conviction, and caused him to discuss those errors with the ardor and solemnity of a self-convicted sinner. His doctrinal progress always was accompanied with new practical light and experience to his own mind, until at last, when he reached the true doctrine of justification by faith without works, he also *felt himself a new creature in Christ Jesus*, rejoiced in *the sense of pardoned sin*, and preached the novel doctrine with all the ardor and self-conviction of one who had himself recently been *plucked as a brand from the everlasting burning*.

The design of our work forbids us to follow the successive steps of this unexampled religious revolution. Our limits allow us at most to enumerate some of the prominent features by which it was distinguished.

The Reformation was not a sudden transition from the midnight darkness of superstition, to the meridian light of divine truth. As all changes of this kind are gradual, so here also the providence of God had for several centuries, progressively, prepared the way for the success which attended the efforts of the great reformers. The influence of Wickliffe in England, and Conrad Stickna and John Milicz in Prague, in the fourteenth century, and of John Huss and Jerome, of the same city, in the fifteenth century, had tended to enlighten the Catholic world, in some degree, on the corruptions of the popes and priests. The positions maintained by these reformers and their followers, known as Hussites and Taborites, were the following, viz.: the unrestricted preaching of God's word; the restoration of the cup to the laity; the divesting of the priesthood of its secular power and wealth; the introduction of a more rigid and scriptural church discipline; the abolition of monasteries, and of images in worship; the rejection of the doctrine of Purgatory and Auricular Confession. Now, as thousands of German students frequented the University of Prague, it is easily perceptible that, returning to their native land, they would disseminate some light not entirely uninfluential in preparing the way for the efforts of the illustrious reformer of Wittenberg and his more perfect work in the succeeding century, especially among those acquainted with the writings of Huss. The priesthood were moreover very generally detested by the masses on account of their immoralities, and by the better classes on account of their ignorance and want of social culture. The papal hierarchy had also become offensive, and a burden to the crowned heads of Europe, who were on that account willing to see it humbled.

The commencement of the public work of Reformation, as is well known, was made by Luther's protest against the sale of papal indulgences vended around Wittenberg by Tetzel, and by his publishing ninety-five theses or propositions, exposing their unscriptural character and destructive influence on the souls of men. But the Reformation properly began some years before in the heart of Luther himself.

When eighteen years of age, in 1505, he entered the monastery, with a terrified conscience for the purpose of saving his own soul. From that time till he published his theses and preached against indulgences, in 1517, the thirtieth year of his age, he was the subject of progressive religious exercises and experience. Soon after his transfer to the monastery at Wittenberg, and his appointment as professor in the University, Dr. Staupitz, the superintendent of the Augustinian monasteries, urged him to direct his attention to preaching. To this request of his beloved superior, Luther yielded, and soon after commenced to preach, first, in the cloister or saloon of the monastery, and afterwards in the parish church of Wittenberg. Here his pulpit performances arrested general attention, even long before he inveighed against indulgences, not only on account of his superior eloquence, but also of their unusual practical excellence, and the remarkable spirituality of his explanations of the doctrines of the church. In the words of Montgomery:

"So felt the young Reformer, when he rose
Within the square, high-fated Wittenberg,
Where the grey walls of St. Augustine's fane
Crumble in low decrepitude and dust,
And from his pulpit piled with simple planks,

Blew the loud trumpet of salvation's truth
Whose echoes yet the heart of empires wake
To fine pulsations, free as Luther loved!
Eye, cheek, and brow with eloquence arrayed
As though the Spirit would incarnate be,
Or mind intense would burn its dazzling way
Through shading matter—like a second Paul,
Flaming with truth, the fearless herald poured
Himself in language o'er the list'ning hearts
Around him! —like a mental torrent ran
The rich discourse, and on that flood of mind
Nearer and nearer to the Lamb's white throne
The soul was wafted: Christ for man,
And man for Christ, and God for all he proved,
And hid himself behind the cross he raised."

After the degree of Doctor of Divinity had been conferred on him, he also commenced lecturing on the *Scriptures in the University*, in 1512. From this time his University instructions assumed more of a religious character. The fame of Aristotle and of the scholastic writers was now gradually supplanted by that of Augustine and the word of God; and he exerted an important and increasing influence on the thousands of students who flocked to hear him, so that he had acquired great celebrity and influence before he publicly commenced the proper work of the Reformation. When he therefore posted up the ninety-five theses, and began to preach and lecture on them, all eyes were fixed upon him, not knowing whereunto this thing would grow. From this time for nine and twenty years, he ceased not to labor and teach in the University and in the pulpit, publicly and privately, by his manly and melodious voice and his prolific pen; filling the country by his numerous pamphlets and books, of which numbers appeared every year, by his extensive correspondence, exerting a widespread influence on learned men, princes, and noblemen of all grades. But most of all did he enlighten the minds of learned and unlearned, of rich and poor, of high and low, by his excellent translation of the word of God into the vernacular language of the land. By this noble work, men of all classes could examine the infallible word of God for themselves, could test the truth of his charges against the corruptions of the Roman hierarchy. Thus was the great work of the Reformation based upon a rock, and a large portion, not only of Germany, but of the other nations of Europe, rescued from the superstitions, the self-delusions and errors of Popery, as well as taught to know and love the pure doctrines of primitive Christianity.

Such and so great was the work, which God accomplished for his church, through the instrumentality of his servants, Luther, and a long catalogue of devoted and noble-hearted fellow-laborers, in Germany and other countries of Europe.

CHAPTER V.

Organization of the different Protestant Denominations of Europe.

THE glorious work of the Reformation was introduced into the different countries of Europe at different times and by different agencies. The peculiar circumstances of each country gave a peculiar direction to the course of events, and thus impressed a peculiar structure and character alike on the work and its results. On the continent the views of Luther moulded the church in Germany, Denmark, Sweden, and Norway, and hence the Lutheran church was established by law in those countries. The doctrines of Zwingli prevailed in the greater part of Switzerland, and those of Calvin in the Cantons of French origin, as also especially in Scotland and some parts of England. These churches also were severally established by the civil governments. In different portions of Germany, Reformed and also Romish churches coexist with the Lutheran, the rights of each being secured and adjusted by the civil law.

Even in Europe, where the civil government prescribes metes and bounds to each of the several denominations, controversies, jealousies, and contentions not unfrequently occur; and in Great Britain, and especially in the United States, where religious freedom is entirely unrestrained, and the right of ecclesiastical secession unlimited, the number of sects and denominations is greatly multiplied.

Hence, whilst contemplating the church of the Redeemer from the time when the Master tabernacled on earth to the present day, we are forcibly struck by the contrast between the manifest unity in the earlier centuries, and the multitude of her divisions since the Reformation. During the former period, the great mass of the orthodox Christian community on earth constituted one universal, *i. e.* catholic church, excepting only several comparatively small clusters of Christians, such as the Donatists and Novàtians. During the earlier centuries, the apostolic and succeeding churches existed under the form of *Independency* or *Congregationalism;* each church having final jurisdiction over its own affairs, aided by voluntary mutual consultations between contiguous churches. Then their union consisted, *neither* in the subjection of the churches, in an entire nation, to one supreme judicatory; much less in the subjection of the entire church on earth to one visible head or pope. Nor did absolute unanimity of religious opinions then exist. But the manifestations of unity in the church consisted, *first,* in unity of *name:* all churches being known as Christian, and only Christian churches, their geographical designation sufficing to distinguish them from each other. *Secondly,* it consisted in unity in the profession of *fundamental* doctrines, expressed most probably in something like the so-called Apostles' Creed. *Thirdly, unity* in the *mutual acknowledgment* of each other's acts of discipline, and finally in *sacramental* and *ministerial communion.*

After the union of Church and State under Constantine the Great, the church was divided according to the political departments of the Roman Empire, being controlled by bishops and patriarchs, and finally, in the seventh century, the entire Western empire was subjected to the ecclesiastical dominion of the pope at Rome. Since the blessed Reformation, the purest portion of God's heritage, the Protestant world is cleft into a multitude of parties, each claiming superior purity, and each maintaining a separate ecclesiastical organization. The separation of the Protestants from the Papal hierarchy was an unavoidable duty; for Rome had poisoned the fountains of truth by her corruptions, and death, or a refusal to drink from her cup, was the only alternative. Babylon the Great was fallen under the divine displeasure, and the voice from heaven must be obeyed, "*Come out of her, my people, that ye be not partakers of her sins,* and that ye receive not her plagues." But that Protestants themselves should afterwards separate from each other; should break communion with those whom they professed to regard as Brethren, and organize entirely independent of each other, was inconsistent with the practice of the apostolic church, and at least in the extent to which it was carried, and the principles on which it was based, detrimental to the interest of the Christian cause.

But it should not be forgotten, that the position thus assumed was, so far as ulterior results are concerned, rather adventitious than designed. The Protestant churches struggled into existence amid circumstances of excitement, oppression, and agitation, both civil and ecclesiastical. This state of things was highly unpropitious, alike to the formation of correct views of church polity in theory, and their introduction in practice. The Reformation itself could not have been effected, except by the aid of the civil arm, which protected its agents from Papal vengeance. A total exclusion of the civil authorities from ecclesiastical action would probably have blasted the Reformation in the bud, even if the views of the earlier reformers had led them to desire such exclusion. Owing partly to these circumstances, and partly to the remains of Papal bigotry still adhering to them, the Protestants in different countries necessarily assumed organizations, not only entirely separate, as in some respects they properly might be, but having little reference to the church as a whole, and calculated to cast into the background the fundamental unity actually existing between them. Without entering into a detail of their origin, it may be interesting to the popular reader to refer to the successive dates of their formation.

The *Lutheran* Church grew up with the Reformation itself, which commenced in 1517. The early history of the one in Germany, Denmark, Sweden and Norway is also the history of the other. The commencement of the church may be dated either from 1520, when Luther renounced his allegiance to popery, by committing the emblems of Papal power, the papal bulls and canons, to the flames; or, more properly, it may be fixed at 1530, when the Reformers presented their confession of faith to the Emperor and Diet at Augsburg.*

* At the present (1867) time the number of Lutheran population is estimated as follows:

In Protestant Germany, . . .	24,000,000
Prussia, ...	5,000,000
	29,000,000

The *German Reformed* church was next established, through the agency of that distinguished servant of Christ, Zwingli. He commenced his public efforts as a Reformer in 1519, by opposing the sale of indulgences by the Romish agent Sampsôn. In 1531, a permanent religious peace was made in Switzerland, securing mutual toleration both to the Reformed and the Catholics, and thus stability was given to this portion of the Protestant church.*

The *Episcopal* church may be dated from 1533, when Henry VIII. renounced his allegiance to the

	29,000,000
In Sweden, ...	3,000,000
Denmark, ...	2,000,000
Norway, ...	1,500,000
Poland and Russia, . . .	2,500,000
Austria, Hungary, Bohemia, . .	1,500,000
United States and Canada, . .	1,000,000
West Indies, ...	100,000
Brazil, ...	100,000
South American States, . . .	50,000
	40,750,000

The Lutheran Church in the United States has 40 Synods, 1573 ministers, 2713 congregations, 300,000 communicants, and a population of about 1,000,000.

* The German Reformed Church has in the United States, 1184 churches, 453 ministers, and 110,760 members. Of the numerical strength of this denomination in Europe, we have been unable to obtain any definite and reliable figures.

Pope, and separated the Church of England from the papal see; although the work of actually reforming the corruptions of this church was accomplished at a later date.*

The *Baptist* church may be referred to the year 1535, when Menno Simon commenced his career; or 1536, when it was regularly organized. It, however, also traces its history back to the ancient Waldenses.†

The *Calvinistic* or *Presbyterian* church, using the phrase to designate the church established by Calvin himself, may be dated at 1536, when he was appointed minister at Geneva; or more properly in 1542, when he established the presbytery there. The *Presbyterian* church in England, Scotland, and America, may be regarded as a continuation of the church founded by this eminent servant of God.‡

* The Episcopal Church in the United States contains 33 Dioceses or Synods, 43 bishops, 2147 ministers, 165,652 members. In England and Wales, in 1851, there were 14,077 Episcopal churches and chapels, and probably about the same number of ministers.

† The Associated Baptist churches in the United States contain 481 Associations, 9659 churches, 6259 ordained ministers, 1171 licentiates, and 776,370 communicants.

The Free-Will Baptists report 125 Associations, 1173 churches, 905 ordained ministers, 165 licentiates, and 51,775 communicants.

‡ The Presbyterian Church proper, is divided into two

The *Congregational* or *Independent* church of modern times, may be dated from 1616, when the first Congregational or Independent church was organized in England by Mr. Jacob.*

The modern *Moravian* church,† or church of *the United Brethren,* may be regarded as originating in 1727, when Count Zinzendorf and Baron Waterville were selected as directors of that fraternity.

The origin of the *Methodist* church‡ may be

separate organizations, popularly known as the Old and the New School Assemblies.

The former reports, for 1866, thirty-five Synods; presbyteries, 176; ministers, 2294; churches, 2608; communicants, 239,236.

New-School Presbyterian Assembly reports for 1866: 23 Synods, 109 presbyteries, 1870 ministers, 115 licentiates, 273 candidates, 161,539 communicants, and 163,242 Sunday School membership.—*Minutes of Assembly for* 1867.

Cumberland Presbyterian churches, 1312; ministers, 1207; members, 113,300. Other minor Presbyterian denominations: churches, 1088; ministers, 868; members, 123,621.

* Congregationalists count 3509 churches, 2902 ministers, and 350,021 members.

† Moravians have 34 churches, 48 ministers, 6334 members, in the United States.

‡ The *Methodist Episcopal Church* has 67 Annual Conferences; the number of local preachers is 8602, travelling preachers, 7576; making a total ministerial force of 16,178. Total membership reported, is, 1,032,184.

traced to 1729, when its honored founder, John Wesley, and Mr. Morgan commenced their meetings for the practical study of the sacred volume.

Numerous other denominations, of minor extent, are found among us, whose principles coincide more or less with those of the churches here specified. All these together constitute the aggregate body of Protestants, and are the great mass of the visible Church of the Redeemer, engaged in promoting his mediatorial reign on earth, and owned in various degrees by the Saviour as his own people.

The following general statistics may be regarded as reliable:

Ecclesiastical Statistics of America

Country.	Total Population.	Protestant.	Roman Catholic.	Total Christians.
Russian America	54,400	....	....	10,700
British America	4,400,913	2,590,000	1,760,000	4,350,000
United States	31,429,891	25,000,000	3,000,000	28,000,000
Mexico	7,661,000	....	7,661,000	7,661,000
Central America	2,227,000	....	2,227,000	2,227,000
South America	21,278,743	50,000	21,200,000	21,250,000
French Possessions	301,323	....	289,000	289,000
Dutch "	85,792	32,600	30,000	62,000
Danish "	47,029	} 55,000	10,000	65,000
Swedish "	18,000	}		
Spanish "	2,032,062	....	2,032,000	2,032,000
Hayti	560,000	10,000	550,000	560,000
Free Indians	319,000	....	....	....
	70,415,153	27,737,600	38,759,000	66,516,600

Religious Denominations in the United States.

Denominations.	Churches.	Ministers.	Members.
African Methodist Episcopal Church	....	....	22,009
" " " Zion Church	....	....	6,820
Baptists:			
Regular	13,178	9,370	1,143,340
Anti-Mission	1,890	892	66,000
Seventh-Day	69	85	7,354
Six Principal	19	17	3,300
Free Will	1,341	1,329	62,707
River Brethren	84	68	7,700
Winebrennerians	289	139	15,400
Dunkers	210	105	22,000
Mennonites	328	273	41,096
Disciples, (Campbellites)	1,890	1,575	330,000
Christian Connection	2,310	1,575	198,000
Congregationalists:			
Orthodox	2,999	2,721	285,021
Unitarian	356	276	33,000
Episcopalians	2,147	2,147	165,652
Friends:			
Orthodox	....	....	59,400
Hicksite	....	....	44,000
German Evangelical Union of the West	....	....	3,300
German Reformed	1,184	453	110,760
Israelites	178	....	220,000
Lutherans	2,713	1,573	297,761
Methodists:			
Episcopal	10,418	7,281	1,010,515
Church South	1,178	2,720	549,663
Protestant	....	....	99,000
Evangelical Association	624	405	52,126
Wesleyan	....	....	23,100
Presbyterians:			
Old School	2,608	2,294	250,332
New School	1,696	1,870	161,539
Cumberland	1,321	1,207	113,300
Reformed	122	59	11,000
" Synod	82	62	7,315
United	497	466	63,323
United Synod of Presbyterian Church	202	122	14,227
Old School (in the Confederate States)			
Associate Synod of North America	49	15	1,112
" " of New York	15	17	1,794
" " of the South	79	84	10,450
Free Presbyterian Synod of the U. States	42	43	4,400
Reformed Protestant Dutch Church	440	450	56,680
Roman Catholics	2,842	2,432	....
Swedenborgians, (New Jerusalem Church)	60	51	5,500
United Brethren, (Moravians)	34	48	6,334
United Brethren in Christ	1,173	1,550	112,841
Universalists	727	949	....

Ecclesiastical Statistics of Europe.

Country.	Population.	R. Catholic.	Protestant.
Portugal	3,923,410	3,913,000	7,000
Spain	16,560,813	16,550,813	10.000
France	37,472,732	35,734,667	1,561,250
Austria, (including Venetia)	35,019,058	27,505,375	3,233,486
Prussia	18,497,458	6,867,574	11,287,448
The other German States (exclusive of Holstein, Lauenburg, Luxemburg, and Limburg	17,046,137	5,587,473	11,075,502
Italy, (including the Papal Territory and San Marino, but exclusive of Venetia)	22,430,000	21,350,000	50,000
Switzerland	2,510,494	1,023,430	1,482,848
Holland, (inclusive of Luxemburg and Limburg)	3,569,456	1,250,000	2,023,000
Belgium	4,731,957	4,600,000	25,000
Great Britain	29,307,199	6,000,000	23,000,000
Denmark Proper, (inclusive of Iceland and the Faroe Islands)	1,673,805	2,000	2,670,000
Schleswig, Holstein, and Lauenburg	1,004,473		
Sweden	3,856,888	4,000	5,463,000
Norway	1,617,564		
Russia, (inclusive of Poland and Finland)	65,819,359	7,020,000	3,940,000
Turkey	16,440,000	640,000	40,000
Greece	1,343,293	45,000	2,000
	282,823,096	138,103,332	65,880,534

CHAPTER VI.

Special History of the Evangelical Lutheran Church.

THE rise and progress of the *Evangelical*, or, as it was subsequently styled, the *Lutheran* Church, as a separate denomination, or branch of the Christian church, were gradual. Its incipient period was December the 10th, 1520, when Luther, after having been summoned by the Pope to recant his alleged errors, committed the papal bull, decretals and canons to the flames, in presence of an immense assemblage of all ranks and orders of people, without the Elster gate of Wittenberg, which was near his residence and the University; thus voluntarily withdrawing from the corrupt church of Rome. He thereby openly renounced his allegiance to the papal chair, and rendered the expected papal bull of excommunication a blow into the air. The second period, from which some have dated the origin of the renovated church, is January 6th, 1521, when the papal bull of excommunication was hurled at Luther by Leo X. The third period is 1530, during the Diet at Augsburg, when the celebrated Confession, or, as it was first termed, *Apology*, was published, and the doctrinal system of the Lutheran Church first *officially* announced to the world. The doctrinal errors of Rome were repudiated *successively* by the great Reformer, as his own convictions of bible truth became clearer; and his followers embraced his amended views as they were progressively published.

The Confession of Augsburg was prepared by Melanchthon, and submitted to Luther after it was composed, and was approved by him. Yet various alterations were subsequently made by Melanchthon. It was not intended as an entire exhibition of the system of doctrines which the reformers had embraced, so much as a statement of doctrines of the ancient church retained by them, with a list of the *principal* abuses which had crept into the Romish church, presented in order to convince the emperor and Diet, that the points of Protestant divergence were neither so numerous nor so great as to make it improper to tolerate them.* "These," say the Confessors in the conclusion of their Confession, "are the *principal* articles which are regarded as disputed.

* See C. Niemeyer's "Melanchthon im Jahre der Augsburgischen Confession." Halle, 1830, passim. See Schmucker's "Vindication of American Lutheranism," pp. 47–54, 74–78.

For, although we might have enumerated many *other corruptions and errors*, yet, in order to avoid prolixity and length, we have mentioned only the *principal*, from which the others can easily be estimated."* From that time the Augsburg Confession was regarded as the most authentic exhibition of the Lutheran doctrines, although the pastors of the church were not required to pledge themselves to all its teachings. The Ecumenical creeds of the earlier centuries were also held in high esteem. Other writings, called forth by transpiring emergencies, also acquired great authority in the church, such as the Apology to the Augsburg Confession by Melanchthon; the Catechisms of Luther, the Smaller one composed for the instruction of the rising generation, whilst the Larger Catechism was for the benefit of the ministers; and the Smalcald Articles, prepared by Luther for submission by the Protestant princes at the expected general council of *Mantua*.

Yet were not any of these documents made absolutely binding on the ministers generally, until *fifty years after the publication of the Augsburg Confession*,

* Dies sind die *fürnehmsten* Artikel, die für streitig geacht werden. Denn wiewohl man *vielmehr Misbräuch und Unrichtigkeit* hätte anziehen *können*, so haben wir doch, die Weitläufigkeit und Länge zu verhüten, allein die fürnehmsten gemeldet, daraus die andern leichtlich zu ermessen." Aug. Confession, Art. XXVIII., p. 69 of Müller's ed.

and *thirty-four years after Luther's death.* During the whole lifetime of the great Reformer himself, and during more than half a century from the origin of the Lutheran Church, her ministry were not bound by an *oath or subscription* to absolute conformity to any human creeds, whilst certain standard works were regarded as fair exponents of the leading doctrines of the Gospel. In no instance did Luther, during his whole life, propose to have the ministry bound to any human creed. The spirit of Luther was, therefore, one of Protestant liberty, and the church, which he was instrumental in founding and developing, during the first half century of her history, occupied substantially the ground, as to creeds, *that our General Synod has done and still does,* requiring assent to the Augsburg Confession, only so far as *fundamentals* are concerned. Hear the language of this fearless and enlightened servant of Christ.

LUTHER'S TESTIMONY ON THE WICKEDNESS AND FOLLY OF ALL ATTEMPTS OF CONSTRAINT IN MATTERS OF FAITH.*

"Whenever we attempt to lay a law upon men that they should believe so and so, then certainly God's Word is not there; if God's Word be not there, it is uncertain whether he desires it; for what he

* *Luther's Works,* vol. xviii. pp. 394, 395.

does not command, we are not certain whether that pleases him; yea, we are certain that it does not please God. For he wishes our faith to be grounded entirely upon his Divine Word, as he says in Matthew xvi., 'On this rock will I build my church,' and in John x., 'My sheep hear my voice and know me, but the voice of a stranger will they not hear, but flee from him.' From this it follows that worldly power drags men to eternal death by such insolent command: for it forces them to believe as right and certainly pleasing to God, what is uncertain, yea, certain that it displeases, because there is no clear Word of God there. Whoever believes as right what is wrong or uncertain, denies the truth, which is God himself, believes in falsehood and error, and holds to be right what is wrong. Therefore it is, in the highest sense, a foolish thing when they say we shall believe the Church, the father and the councils, when there is no Word of God there. They are the devil's Apostles who could give such commands, and not the Church; for the Church does not command, unless she is certain that it is God's Word, as St. Peter says: 'Let him that speaketh, speak as the oracles of God.' But they are far from proving that the determinations of the councils are the oracles of God. . . . . . No one can command the soul, unless he knows how to direct the way to heaven. This no man can do, but God alone. Therefore in the matters which concern the salvation of the soul, nothing but the Word of God is to be taught and received. . . . . . Tell me now, how much wit must the head have who would propose law at a place where he has no authority? Who would not consider it foolish to command the moon to shine when we please? How would it appear for those at Leipsig to lay a command upon us at Wittenberg, or for us at Wittenberg upon those at Leipsig? . . . . . Therefore every man believes as he believes, at his own peril, and must see to it that his faith is right. For as little as another can descend to hell or ascend to heaven for me, so little can he believe or not believe for me; and as little as he can lock or unlock heaven for me, so little can he drive me to faith or unbelief. As then it lies upon each one's conscience how he believes or does not believe, provided he does not thereby disturb temporal government, it must also be satisfied and attend to its own business, and let each one believe thus or so, as he can and will, and urge no one with force. For it is a free work which concerns faith, to which no man can be forced. *Yea, it is a divine work in the spirit.* Let it not be said that external power can force or produce it. It is therefore the expression of common sense, when Augustine says: 'We cannot and should not drive any man to faith.'

"These miserable, blind people do not see what a

vain and impossible thing they undertake. Violently as they command, and though they almost rave, they cannot bring the people further than to follow them with the mouth and the hand; the heart they cannot force, though they tear themselves in pieces; for it is a true proverb, '*Gedanken sind zollfrey;*' thoughts are free. What is the result, then, when they endeavor to force the people to believe in the heart—which is impossible—but that they drive weak consciences with force to lie, to deceive, and to speak otherwise than they believe in the heart. They burden themselves with horrible sin of others. For all the lying and false confessing which such weak consciences do return upon him who forces them, it would be better—though the people should err—to let them err, than to drive them to lie, and to speak contrary to what is in their heart; for it is not right to prevent a less evil by a greater.

Page 408. "Over against all this we say, let the councils conclude and determine concerning temporal things, or concerning things not yet expounded; but where God's Word and will are clear, we will not wait for the determinations of council or Church, but fear God, go forth and do it, without thinking, whether there be council or not. For I will not wait to see whether councils will conclude, whether I shall believe in God the Father and Maker of heaven and earth, in his only-begotten Son Jesus

Christ our Lord, &c., nor what I am to believe, in regard to open, clear, and certain parts of Scripture which are necessary and useful to me. For if councils should delay, and I should die in the meantime, what would become of my soul, if it should not know already, but must wait for the councils to determine what it is to believe, when faith is immediately necessary."

Happy would it be, if the ultra-symbolists of our church, who manifest so warm a zeal for our immortal Luther, could rise to the spirit of the great Reformer, and taking a lesson from his example, chasten their zeal by the knowledge it would afford them. Would that they could ponder the fact, that, though Luther published several writings containing a condensed view of Scripture doctrine, such as his Catechisms, and the Smalcald Articles, and added his name to them, he never, *no never, bound himself or others to receive them,* or any other uninspired productions, as his directory of faith. No, not a single one, even of his own writings, did he invest with this authority. Although so great a man, and so highly favored of God, he well knew and acknowledged his own fallibility. He knew that if it were proper to make his writings binding on others, the productions of other men, equally learned and pious, of earlier and of later ages, would have the same claim; and then might it be said, "that the world could not contain (understand and reconcile) the (mass of symbolic) books that should be written." Hence no uninspired books are in themselves binding on others, except by voluntary assent. It is the right and duty of the Church in every age to profess her own views of Bible truth; but to exact assent from others only to the great concurrent views of fundamental truth, which the wise and good of all ages find in the Scriptures, and consider necessary to fraternal co-operation. These may be regarded as certainly taught in God's Word, and be employed in subjection to that Word, in the admission of church-members.

As to forms of Government and Discipline, the Reformers were unable to carry out their own convictions. They regarded *parity* of ministers as the primitive mode of government. But the Protestant princes, who had protected their life and liberties against their papal enemies, assumed the power of regulating the external affairs of the Church, and introduced some inequality on the ground of human expediency. They appointed a mixed commission of civil and ecclesiastical officers, under the name of *Consistorium,* to make all necessary arrangements touching public worship, the appointment and succession of pastors, &c., thus again placing the Church under the control of the State. As to church *Discipline,* Luther early saw the necessity of a Scriptural discipline; but also confessed at a later day his inability to carry his views into effect. Some few regulations of discipline were introduced into the various Church Directories (Kirchen-Ordnungen), adopted by the churches in different countries; but nothing like a *complete Scriptural church discipline* was ever adopted in any part of our Church until 1823, when the General Synod of our American Lutheran Church published theirs, which has now been circulated over our entire country with their English Hymn-book.*

In regard to *modes and forms of worship*, Luther was opposed to all coercion. "The heart," he says, "is the thing with which we must worship God." "As the external forms of worship neither justify nor condemn us before God, and as they, if prescribed as a law, may easily give rise to the superstitious belief that these external forms constitute the worship of God, and are necessary to salvation, and that the neglect of them is sinful, *therefore the externals of worship should be free, and without coer-*

* The first VII Chapters of the *Formula*, relating to congregations, were prepared by the present writer, and adopted by the Synod of Maryland and Virginia, in 1823, at Cumberland, Md., then adopted by the General Synod, and recommended to all the churches. The Constitution for District Synods was prepared by the same hand, and adopted by the General Synod at Hagerstown, in 1829.

cion." In general, two different tendencies were manifested during the formation of the Lutheran Church. Some advocated the rejection of all rites and ceremonies not found in the Scriptures, whilst others evinced a more ritualistic spirit, preferring to retain all the customs of the Romish Church which were not clearly inconsistent with God's word. Each section of the Church was finally permitted to follow its own judgment in this matter, and the principle was adopted, and expressed in the Augsburg Confession, "That it is not necessary that the same human traditions—that is, rites and ceremonies instituted by men, should be everywhere observed."—*Art. VII.* Each kingdom and principality, and even city, *had its own liturgy;* and whilst they all agreed in essential features, they differed widely in those things not decided in Scripture. The *public worship* was in a great measure restored to its primitive apostolic simplicity and spirituality, and consisted in *preaching* the Word, *singing, prayer,* and the *administration of the sacraments.* The catechetical instruction of the rising generation was universally required. The greater part of the Romish festivals were rejected. Luther was, indeed, at first in favor of discarding all the festivals, except the Lord's Day,—thus agreeing with the position maintained by Calvin and Zwingli. In his discourse on "Good Works,' in 1520. Luther remarks:—"All the festivals ought to be laid aside, and the Sabbath alone be retained; or, the festivals should be removed to the Sabbath."* At a later day he changed his opinion, and maintained that, in addition to the Lord's Day, several other festivals might be observed. In the churches of the General Synod, only those few festivals are observed which commemorate the fundamental facts of Christianity, viz., Christmas, Good Friday, Easter, Ascension Day, and Whitsuntide. The festival of the Reformation, to commemorate the renovated Church of Christ, is also observed by many of our churches.

Thus did the mother Church of the Reformation gradually assume definite and settled lineaments. This portraiture, however, did not, in all respects, reach the ideal at which the reformers aimed; yet had a great work of God been achieved, and many millions of souls been rescued from the dominion of Papal ignorance and superstition, and restored to the purity of gospel truth. Nor would the renovated Church have failed to extend its limits into other portions of the Germanic empire, had it not been for the union of Church and State: "For," says Dr. Mosheim, "that very religious peace, which was the instrument of its stability and independence,

* Luther's Works, (Walch's ed.) vol. x. pp. 1630 and 1647. Zwingli, Explanation of the XXV Article. Calvin's Institutes, Lib. ii. c. 8, &c.; and Herzog's Encycl., vol. iv., p. 380.

set bounds at the same time to its progress in the empire, and effectually prevented" its further extension there. In the Diet of Augsburg, assembled in the year 1555, in order to execute the treaty of Passau, the several States that had already embraced the Lutheran religion were confirmed in the full enjoyment of their religious liberty. To prevent, as far as possible, the farther progress of the Reformation, Charles V. stipulated for the Catholics the famous ecclesiastical reservation; by which it was decreed, that "if any archbishop, bishop, prelate, or other ecclesiastic, should in time to come renounce the faith of Rome, his dignity and benefice should be forfeited, and his place be filled by the chapter or college possessed of the power of election." * Here, then, is the response to the oft-proposed inquiry, Why did the work of the Reformation so abruptly terminate, and why has the Protestant Church in Germany remained stationary for three centuries?

For half a century after the publication of the Augsburg Confession, the Church as a whole was free from symbolic coercion. In 1580, the *Form of Concord,* together with all the other documents referred to, were combined into one volume; and by order of Augustus of Saxony, and subsequently other

* See Dr. McLean's translation of Mosheim's History, vol. iii. p. 215, note K., by the translator.

civil authorities, was enforced in different kingdoms of Germany by the requisition of an oath from every minister in the land. This measure, though doubtless prompted by a desire to promote harmony and peace, was unwise, un-Lutheran, and unscriptural; as these books embraced a great many minor points of doctrinal opinion, which are not clearly revealed in Scripture, and are not necessary either to harmonious co-operation, or to the purity of the Church. For Paul admonishes us "to receive the brother (that is, him whom we regard as a brother in Christ), who is weak in *the* faith, (or, erroneous in some of his views of *the* faith,) but not for doubtful disputation." A short creed seems to be necessary in order to preserve the purity of the Church, and had the Augsburg Confession alone been made binding, instead of the whole mass of symbolic books, equal in bulk to the Old Testament, the peace of the Church would have been better preserved, liberty of conscience have been respected, and the Church of the Reformation been far more widely extended than she now is. But, controlled as the Church then was, and still is in Europe, she had no opportunity in her collective capacity to influence this subject then, or to effect any reform since.

But the attempt to enforce the reception of the whole mass of the symbolical books proved a signal failure; for the rulers of different kingdoms and principalities in which the influence of Luther predominated, and the Lutheran type of theology prevailed, wisely refused to accept some of these books as symbolical; whilst they regarded them as in other respects valuable productions.

As it is important that the facts connected with the failure of this Collection of Symbols, or Book of Concord, to gain general acceptance in the Lutheran Church, should be known to her intelligent laity, we here introduce them from our History of the American Lutheran Church, to which the reader is referred who desires a more extended discussion of the subject.

I. The Form of Concord, published 1580, was rejected by the following Lutheran nations, principalities, dukedoms, &c., and yet no one ever attempted to deny their right to the name *Lutheran.*

1. *The kingdom of Denmark.* "The king, though invited to adopt it, refused to do so, by advice of his clergy, who disapproved of it, because peace and unity of doctrine prevailed in his dominions, and he feared its introduction would create strife and divisions. And so bitterly was he opposed to it himself, that he *took the copy (decorated with gold and pearls) sent him from Germany, cast it into the fire, and made it a capital offence* to introduce and publish it in the kingdom." Kœllner's Symbolik, vol. i. pp. 575, 576.

And though at a subsequent period it acquired some popularity, and was practically used, it was never publicly acknowledged as a symbol. See Baumgarten's Erlæuterungen zum Concordienbuch, pp. 184, 185. Mosheim's Eccles. Hist., vol. iii. p. 155, Murdock's edition.

We add the testimony of Shubert's celebrated work on the Ecclesiastical and Educational Institutions of Sweden, as summarily given by Kœllner. After repeating in full the oath of ordination, which mentions, in addition to the three ancient creeds, only the Augsburg Confession, and refers to the Liber Concordiæ as illustration of it, Kœllner adds this remark: "Upon the whole, the case of Sweden is like that of Denmark and of Holstein. It was from the beginning customary to bind one's self to the symbolical books, which were not adopted until after the time of the Reformation, *only in as far as they were believed to agree with the holy Scriptures.*" In later times, it is customary in public documents, instead of the phrase, "the *Lutheran doctrine*," to use the more appropriate expression, "the pure *evangelical doctrine.*" Kœllner's Symbolik, I., p. 122.

2. *The kingdom of Sweden* did not receive it during the first thirteen years after its publication. Hear the testimony of that ultra-Lutheran historian Guericke, (Symbolik, 2d edition, pp. 112, 113.) "And if Denmark and *Sweden,* stopping at a still

more youthful age in regard to Confessions, did not concede proper symbolical authority to the Apology to the Augsburg Confession, or to the Smalcald Articles, or the Larger Catechism of Luther, (and in Sweden not even the Smaller Catechism,) they would naturally be still less willing formally to acknowledge the Form of Concord." Guericke, Symb., pp. 112, 113. Still at a later period, in 1593, the Form of Concord received a *tolerably* formal acknowledgment, (ziemlich förmliche Anerkennung.)

3. *Hessia* rejected it.

4. *Pomerania* rejected it.

5. *Holstein* rejected it for more than half a century.

6. *Anhalt;* and the cities of *Strasburg, Frankfort a. M., Speier, Worms, Nürenberg, Magdeburg, Bremen, Dantzic,* &c., &c. Kœllner, p. 577.

II. The Smalcald Articles, published in 1537, were rejected by *Sweden* and *Denmark.* In Sweden, the symbolic books generally are now regarded as an authorized explanation of the Lutheran faith; yet the "Symbolical Books of the *Danish* church, lately published, like those of the *Swedish* church in 1644, (entitled Confession of the *Swedish* faith, approved by the council at Upsal in 1593,) contains only the three ecumenical confessions; namely, the so-called Apostles' Creed, the Nicene and the Atha-

7

nasian Creeds, and the Augsburg Confession, to which the Danish collection adds the Smaller Catechism of Luther. Both these collections, however, exclude the *Smalcald Articles.* Guericke's Symb., p. 67, and his History, p. 807, 1st edition.

III. The Apology to the Augsburg Confession was denied official symbolic authority by Sweden and Denmark. Guericke, sup. cit.

IV. The Larger Catechism of Luther was denied formal symbolic authority in Sweden and Denmark. Guericke, sup. cit.

V. Even the Smaller Catechism of Luther was not received as symbolic in Sweden; yet in both these kingdoms they are highly respected, and the Smaller Catechism, if we mistake not, is used for the instruction of youth. Guericke, p. 113.

Here then we have the historical facts, the greater part of them well known indeed to those who are familiar with the history of our Church in Europe; but, for the benefit of others, proved by the authority of the accurate Kœllner, and of that bigoted Old-Lutheran, Prof. Guericke.

In short, we find that the declaration of Dr. Hase is literally true, when he says the *Augsburg Confession is the only symbolic book, which has been acknowledged by the whole Lutheran Church.* Hutterus Redivivus, p. 116, § 50. And it is certain that much more frequent and important deviations from the Augsburg Confession would have been avowed, if the peace of Augsburg, in 1555, had not guaranteed toleration to the Protestant princes *only so long as they and their theologians adhered to the Augsburg Confession;* and if the Papists and especially the *Jesuits had not watched* even every verbal deviation, and used it to excite the Romish Emperor to withdraw his protection, and to put down Protestantism by fire and sword, which efforts actually eventuated in the thirty years' war. It is well known that even during Luther's lifetime, Melanchthon, Cruciger and others, disapproved of a part of the Augsburg Confession, and yet Luther would not suffer them to leave Wittenberg, or the communion of the Lutheran Church, when they on one occasion expressed a willingness to do so, if they could not deviate from Luther's views without denunciation from several of his followers. In all ages of the Lutheran church, there have been among her ablest divines some who dissented, at least privately, from Luther's opinion, *that the real or true body and blood of Christ are present in the Eucharist, and are received by the communicant,* as taught in the Augsburg Confession. And Guericke himself admits, what is indeed matter of general notoriety, not merely that the theologians, but that *the whole Lutheran church in Germany had rejected this doctrine before* 1817, when the union of the Lutheran and Reformed churches was effected in some parts of that country.*

The Lutheran Church has had various vicissitudes, both prosperous and adverse, in the three centuries of her history, and at this day she still forms the *most numerous body of Protestants in the world.* Within her pale, every phase of genuine piety has been developed, and thousands of the noblest and the best of men, known to the annals of Christianity, have lived and labored and died. And here also, every phase of rationalism and infidelity has been found, and proved the utter inability of the most extended creeds to exclude unbelievers from the Church. It

* Even Melanchthon altered the Xth Article of the Augsburg Confession; and, according to the historian Gottfried Arnold, *Luther made but little objection.* But in 1536 Luther himself concluded a treaty or agreement with the Swabian and Swiss churches, at Wittenberg, on the basis of the *Altered* Confession. See Arnold's Ketzer und Kirchengeschichte, vol. I., p. 810; also, *Dr. Heppe's* Confessional Development of the (*Altprotestantische*) *Primitive Protestant Church of Germany*, pp. 110, 111, &c.

It is also worthy of note, that seven years after the Augsburg Confession had been published, namely, in 1537, the Protestant princes directed their theologians at the convention in Torgau, to examine that Confession by the Scriptures, and to alter whatever might be found in it inconsistent with that infallible rule. See Dr. Tittmann's "Die Evangelische Kirche," Leipsic, 1831, page 3.

remained for the churches of the Evangelical Lutheran General Synod in the United States, where Church and State are happily separate, and the rights of both are legally secured, to return to the principle of the earlier ages, and rising above the sectarian influence of three centuries, to cast off the yoke of symbolic bondage, and restore to our ministry that liberty wherewith Christ hath made them free, and which they enjoyed during the lifetime of Luther. This they did by pledging them only to the *fundamental doctrines* of the Bible, as taught in the mother symbol of Protestantism, the *Augsburg Confession*, avowed before the Diet of Augsburg in the year 1530. By this position, the doctrinal basis of the American Lutheran Church was officially announced to the world. Thus, also, do they reject the contrary extreme of neglecting to require definite assent, even to the fundamental doctrines of the Bible, as was done by the synods of Pennsylvania and New York, at the time when the General Synod of our Church was formed in 1820, and for twenty years before and afterwards.

The principal divines and preachers, who reflected honor on the Lutheran Church in the sixteenth century, besides Luther and Melanchthon, who towered above all the rest, were Chemnitz, Brentius, Flacius, Urban Regius, Major, Amsdorf, Sarcerius, Matthesius, Wigand, Lambert, Jacob Andreä, Chyträus,

Selneccer, Bucer, Strigelius, Spangenberg, Hesshusen, Westphal, Osiander, and others.

During the *seventeenth century,* the rigid symbolism fostered by the Book of Concord of the previous age, gradually degenerated into a lifeless formalism, which expended the energies of the Church in intolerant controversy, whilst the interests of practical piety were, in a great measure, neglected. The *Thirty Years' War* also, waged by the Austrian Emperor against the Protestant nations of Germany, at the instigation of the Jesuits and the Papal hierarchy, spread the most lamentable desolation over the country; and calling into action the vindictive passions of the heart, greatly demoralized the land. God, however, who watches with parental care over his people, did not forsake them entirely, but raised up, at different times, an Arndt, a Spener, a Franke, as shining and burning lights, to dispel the surrounding darkness, and restore to his Church the light and heat of divine truth and grace. About the close of the 17th and *beginning of the 18th century,* revivals, of the most extraordinary and long-continued power and extent, attended the labors of these distinguished servants of the Lord, and made thousands of the congregations in Germany and elsewhere bud and blossom as the rose.

The principal divines and preachers of the 17th century were Aeg. and Nic. Hunnius, John and

John Ernest Gerhard, G. and F. Calixtus, Olearius, F. Baldwin, the Carpzovs, the Lysers, M. Walther, J. V. Andreæ, Sol. Glass, Theod. Hackspan, J. Weller, John Musæus, J. C. Danhauer, John Arndt, the Meisners, Aug. Pfeiffer, Seb. Schmidt, C. Kortholt, Osiander, P. J. Spener, &c.

During the 18th century the Lutheran Church produced a very large number of men, who were ornaments to the Church as well as to her learned institutions. A few only can find room here: Phil. James Spener, Ittig, Gottfried Arnold, Aug. Hermann Franke, Jno. A. Fabricius, J. Francis Buddeus, J. James Rambach, I. C. Wolf, I. Gustavius Reinbeck, Joach. Lange, E. S. Cyprian, J. Alb. Bengel, John Lawrence Mosheim, Sieg. James Baumgarten, Ch. Matth. Pfaff, J. H. Fresenius, C. Aug. Heumann, E. Pantoppidan, J. G. Carpzov, S. Urlsperger, J. E. Shubert, John Geo. Walch, C. Aug. Crusius, J. A. Danz, J. Porst, P. Anthon, John Henry, Christ. Benedict, and J. David Michaelis, Rieger, Mich. Lilienthal, Ernesti, C. W. F. Walch, Spalding, Storr, and Jerusalem.

In the present century we may specify Noesselt, Zachariæ, Griesbach, Augusti, Marheinecke, Less, Koppe, Dœderlein, Morus, Eichhorn, Seiler, Henke, Reinhard, J. G. Rosenmüller, Plank, Geo. Christ. Knapp, Schleusner, Stäudlin, Süskind, Ammon, Tittman, Kuinoel, Bretschneider, Berthold, Gesenius,

Winer, Giesseler, De Wette, Dräsecke, Harms, Neander, Wiggers, Steudel, Tholuk, Dorner, Jul. Miller, Twesten, Olshausen, Nitch, Ullman, Harless, Niedner, Gosner, Hofacker, Thomasius, Hoffman, Delitsch, Kœllner, Ehrenfeuchter, Guericke, Hase, Schwartz Luthardt, Beck, Landerer, Palmer, Kliefoth, and Rudelbach.

During the *latter half of the 18th century*, the infidelity of England and France found its way into Germany, and greatly corrupted the literary and theological institutions of the land of Luther. But since the year 1817, when Claus Harms published his theses against *rationalism*, a salutary reaction has been taking place throughout not only Germany, but nearly all Protestant Europe, the doctrines of the Bible are again taught in their fundamental purity; the cause of piety has been making steady progress, and millions are rejoicing in the consciousness of the power of divine grace in their hearts. Christians have waked up to a sense of their obligation to labor for the glory of God, and the salvation of men. Every form of Christian benevolence finds open hearts and willing hands, and thousands of missionaries are now laboring in the foreign field, to teach unto the gentiles the unsearchable riches of Christ.

Some of these missionaries, emanating from Halle, the chief seat of the *pietistic revivals*, were sent in

1742, and later, to the United States, to labor among the German Lutherans,* who had emigrated to this country at different times during the earlier part of that century. Some German Lutherans had come from Holland to New York before 1664, when the colonial dominion passed from the Hollanders to the British.† Under the former, the Lutherans were not allowed to celebrate public worship, and were compelled to hold their meetings in private. But the English government, without any hesitation, granted the liberty of holding public worship to our forefathers. Prior to this time, some Swedish Lutherans had emigrated to this country, and in 1630 settled, and formed churches on the Delaware, within the present bounds of the States of New Jersey and Delaware.‡

In 1642, Luther's Smaller Catechism was translated by the Rev. Campanius, a Swedish minister, into the language of the neighboring Indians. The first Lutheran minister in New York, whose name has reached us, was Jacobus Fabricius, in 1669, in which year the first Lutheran Church was built in that city. The first Lutheran missionary sent to Pennsylvania from Halle, was Henry Melchior Mühlenberg, a man distinguished alike for learning, for

* Hallische Nachrichten, passim.

† Lutheran Herold, vol. iii. p. 7.

‡ Clay's Annals of the Swedes.

piety, for liberality, and zeal in the Master's cause. So well directed, extensive, and long-continued were his labors and success, in building up the Lutheran Church in this country, that, although several other ministers had been here and labored some years before him, in Pennsylvania, and Reinbeck, New York, he is justly regarded as its chief founder. Among his earliest co-laborers and successors, were Brunholtz, Schaum, Nic. Kurtz, Handschuh, William Kurtz, Voigt, Krug, Schultze, Bager, Helmuth, Schmidt, Kunze, G. H. E. Mühlenberg, Wildbahn, Streit, Jung, Gœring, Melsheimer, D. Kurtz, J. G. Schmucker, Lochman, Endress, &c. The *emigration of Germans to Pennsylvania* commenced soon after 1680, when Charles II. bestowed the grant of Pennsylvania to William Penn.

In 1684, as Pastorius in his Geography of Pennsylvania, published in 1700 at Frankfurt and Leipsic, informs us, there were 4000 Christians of different denominations residing in this State.

In 1687–9, many hundreds of German families emigrated to Pennsylvania.

In 1710, about 3000 families, chiefly from the Palatinate, and Lutherans by profession, arrived at New York, sent on from England by Queen Ann.

In 1727, German emigration to Pennsylvania continued to increase from the Palatinate, from Würtemberg, Darmstadt, &c.

In 1730, 150 families settled at Schoharie, New York.

1730–42, the Swedish pastors sometimes officiated in the German language for the German ministers.

1733, Lutherans emigrated from Saltzburg, in Bavaria, to Georgia. In this year a Lutheran church was erected at York, Pennsylvania.

1735, some Lutheran families settle in Spotsylvania, now Madison County, Virginia.

Thus the stream of emigration continued to flow with greater or less rapidity, and with various fluctuations, until the present time, (1867.) The Germans, moreover, being a robust, healthy nation, not enervated by luxury and indolence, increased with unsurpassed rapidity, and became an important element in our national population. In 1820, when the Constitution of the General Synod was formed, there were 140 Lutheran ministers in this country, and five Synods, viz., the Synod of Pennsylvania and neighboring States, the Synod of New York, the Synod of North Carolina, the Synod of Ohio, and the Synod of Maryland and Virginia, organized October 11, 1820, together constituting our entire Church in America. The Synod of West Pennsylvania was resolved on in 1824, and formally organized in 1825.

In the earliest period of our American Lutheran Church, an intimate and very friendly relation subsisted between our fathers and the Swedish Lutherans on the one hand, and the Church of England —as it was called before the Revolution—on the other. The Swedish and German Lutheran ministers occasionally worshipped together, and a friendly understanding long continued to prevail. But the limited number of Swedes soon brought them into closer contact with the English language; whilst the Germans constituted a community by themselves, and their ministers long pursued the mistaken policy of resisting the introduction of the English tongue into the services of the sanctuary. The Episcopalians promptly tendered ministerial aid to the Swedes, whenever desired, and thus, as emigration from the mother country soon ceased, gradually swallowed up the few existing Swedish churches, which had become almost entirely anglicized before the German Lutherans had allowed any English preaching. The prevalence of diocesan episcopacy in the Church in Sweden, probably also in some degree favored the preference of its members for the Protestant Episcopal Church.

OVERTURES OF THE EPISCOPAL CHURCH FOR UNION BETWEEN THEM AND OUR EARLY FATHERS.

Although our Church had no diocesan episcopacy in Germany, and our fathers never favored its introduction here they thought favorably of the Episcopal Church as a whole. Some of them favored the habit of considering it as the *English Lutheran* Church, and encouraged their anglicized offspring to unite with that body, instead of erecting English Lutheran churches. Thus, one of the sons of the patriarch Mühlenberg entered the Episcopal ministry, and others of his lay descendants connected themselves with that Church, as did his great-grandson, the present excellent William Augustus Mühlenberg, senior pastor of an Episcopal Church in New York. A portion of the family of the venerable Dr. Kunze, of New York, and that of Dr. Helmuth, of Philadelphia, have also been absorbed in the Episcopal Church. In 1763, the Rev. Messrs. Peters and Ingliss, of the Episcopal Church, Philadelphia, were present at the meeting of the Lutheran Synod in that place. In the earlier part of the present century, an offer was also made by Bishop White, of the Episcopal Church, at a meeting of the Pennsylvania Synod, for a union of that body with the Episcopal Church, but it was respectfully declined.*

In the year 1821, a committee of the Episcopal Church attended a meeting of the Synod of North Carolina, to confer on some plan to promote friendly

* The written proposition referred to is doubtless still in the archives of said Synod, and was often seen by the father of the present writer, the Rev. Dr. J. G. Schmucker, then Secretary of that body.

relations between the two Churches; and an arrangement was adopted, according to which any Lutheran minister should be entitled to a seat in the Episcopal Convention of North Carolina, with the privilege of voting on all subjects that did not specially appertain to the Episcopal Church, and *vice versa.*

Rev. Dr. Kunze, in his preface to a volume of sermons published in 1797, says: "I have these twenty-four years, *i. e.*, as long as I have instructed students of divinity for my Church, held this and no other language to them; and it was in consequence of this subsisting union between the Lutheran and English (Episcopal) Church, that the Evangelical Lutheran Consistory, held at Reinbeck, New York, on the 1st of September, 1797, adopted the following resolution: 'That on account of the intimate connexion existing between the English Episcopal and the Lutheran Churches, and the identity of their doctrine, and the near alliance of their Church discipline, this consistory (Synod?) will never acknowledge a newly erected Lutheran Church, merely English, in places where the members may partake of the services of the said English Episcopal Church.'"

This state of feeling also greatly retarded the introduction of the English language, and the education of English ministers in our Church, and involved the loss of a large portion of our best Lutheran material to our American Church. See Evangelical Review, Gettysburg, April, 1856.

These facts furnish a demonstrative evidence, if any more were needed, that the patriarchs of our American Church were not so contracted as some of their professed ultra-symbolic followers. These regard the whole mass of symbolic books as essential to the perfection of the Church of Christ; whilst the former were willing that their *own children should forsake those books* and accept one brief creed, the Thirty-Nine Articles of the Episcopal Church, in their stead. Oh! that these dear brethren could rise to the magnanimity and liberality of their forefathers, and learn practically to distinguish between the essentials and non-essentials of Christianity,—between the fundamental doctrines held in common by all evangelical denominations, and the non-fundamentals, in regard to which the different Churches differ, and yet enjoy the manifest tokens of the Divine blessing on their worship, as well as prove by their works that the Spirit of God dwells in them.

It is, however, to be regretted that, during the last half century, the great body of Episcopalians have become more High-Church and sectarian. On the other hand, the Lutherans have, by continued study of God's Word, been confirmed in the views of Luther and Lutheran theologians generally, of the primitive parity of the ministry, and independence of the churches, and, with a few exceptions, have become increasingly hostile to long liturgies.

PROPOSED UNION OF THE LUTHERAN AND GERMAN REFORMED CHURCHES.

During the previous decennium, repeated efforts had been made to unite the Lutherans and the German Reformed of our land, especially as the doctrinal diversities of the two Churches had almost entirely disappeared, and the membership of both was very generally intermarried. The first definite measure tending towards this end, was

THE PROPOSED UNITED LUTHERAN AND REFORMED THEOLOGICAL SEMINARY.

In accordance with these views, the Synod of Pennsylvania, in 1819,* "appointed the Rev. Drs. J. G. Schmucker, Lochman, Mühlenberg, and Ernst, as a committee to confer with a similar committee of the German Reformed Synod, and devise a plan for a united Theological Seminary for the two denominations." If the Pennsylvania Synod had differed materially from the views of the German Reformed, would they have desired to unite with them in erecting a joint Seminary?

* See Minutes of Pennsylvania Synod for 1819, &c.
Also, J. A. Probst's "Die Wiedervereinigung der Lutheraner und Reformirten." Allentown, 1826.

AN ENTIRE UNION OF BOTH CHURCHES PROPOSED.

In 1822, at the meeting in Germantown, the Pennsylvania Synod *unanimously* adopted the following resolution, on motion of Drs. Endress and Mühlenberg:

"*Resolved*, That a committee be appointed by this Synod to deliberate in the fear of God on the propriety of a proposition for a general union of our Church in this country with the Evangelical Reformed Church, and also on the possibility and most suitable method of carrying this resolution into effect." p. 16 of their Minutes for 1822.

UNANIMOUS DECLARATION OF PENNSYLVANIA SYNOD.

When the Synod of Pennsylvania, at the meeting of 1823, at Lebanon, felt it a duty to yield to the popular clamor excited for selfish purposes by some political demagogues and a renegade German layman, who, it is believed, fled from justice in his native country, and here published a slanderous book against the Synod, and hawked it about from house to house, that body, by an almost unanimous vote, adopted the following declaration of sentiments in the preamble to their resolutions: "We beheld large and beautiful congregations of brethren (the Reformed) who labor with us in the same spirit and with the same view in proclaiming the doctrines of

Jesus, and discharging the duties of the office of reconciliation, who often in the same house labor, teach and worship the same Lord in the same manner and for the same purpose. We gave utterance, as it were, from afar to the wish, dictated by love, to enter into a closer union with these our German Evangelical Protestant brethren, and termed it *a union of the German Protestant Church.* But our own brethren (members) have misapprehended us," &c. p. 15 of their Minutes for 1823. If then the members of this respectable body know their own doctrinal views, these words contain a declaration that they agreed substantially with those of the Reformed, who never received the peculiarities of the Augsburg Confession, such as the presence of the body and blood of the Saviour in the Eucharist, &c., and thus they confirm the declaration of Rev. Probst, that the members of the Pennsylvania Synod generally had rejected this doctrine.

SYNOD OF PENNSYLVANIA, AGAIN.

Although it is a well-known fact that this respectable body has not, for about half a century, until of late years, required assent to anything more than the Bible, not one of the former symbolical books being ever named at licensure or ordination, as may be seen even from the Liturgy of 1818; and although her merely fundamental accordance in fact with the Augsburg Confession is included in the general testimony of Drs. Hazelius, Bachman, Lochman, Krauth, Lintner,* &c., presented in former articles, it will be interesting to hear additional evidence.

Testimony of Rev. John Aug. Probst, who was a member of that Synod from 1813 until his recent death, and well acquainted with the sentiments of his brethren, in a work published in 1826, for the express purpose of promoting a formal and complete union of the German Reformed and Lutheran Churches in America, entitled, "Reunion of the Lutherans and Reformed," argues throughout on the supposition that there was no material difference of doctrinal views between them, the Lutherans having relinquished the *bodily presence,* and the Reformed, unconditional election. Speaking of the supposed obstacles to such union, he remarks: "The doctrine of unconditional election cannot be in the way. This doctrine has long since been abandoned; for there can scarcely be a single German Reformed preacher found who regards it as his duty to defend this doctrine. Zwingli's more liberal, rational, and scriptural view of this doctrine, *as well as of the Lord's Supper,* has become the *prevailing one among Lutherans* and Reformed, and it has been deemed

* See Schmucker's History of the Lutheran Church in America, Chapter VI., pp. 200, &c.

proper to abandon the view of both Luther and Calvin on the subject of both these doctrines." p. 74.

Again: "The whole mass of the old Confessions was occasioned by the peculiar circumstances of those troublous times, has become obsolete by the lapse of ages, and is yet valuable only as matter of *history*. Those times and circumstances have passed away, and our situation, both in regard to political and ecclesiastical relations, is entirely changed. We are therefore not bound to these books, but only to the Bible. For what do the unlearned know of the Augsburg Confession, or the Form of Concord, of the Synod of Dort," &c. p. 76.

Again: "Both churches (the Lutheran and Reformed) advocate the evangelical liberty of judging for themselves, and have one and the same ground of their faith, the Bible. Accordingly, both regard the Gospel as their exclusive rule of faith and practice, and are forever opposed to all violations of the liberty of conscience." p. 76.

Finally: "All enlightened and intelligent preachers of both Churches agree, that there is much in the former symbolical books (or confessions of faith) that must be stricken out as antiquated and contrary to common sense, and be made conformable with the Bible, and that we have no right to pledge ourselves to the mere human opinions of Luther, or

Calvin, or Zwingli, and that we have but one master, Christ. Nor is any evangelical Christian bound to the interpretations which Luther or Calvin, or any other person may place on the words of Christ; but each one has the right to interpret them according to the dictates of his own conscience." p. 80. "Inasmuch as all educated ministers of the Lutheran and Reformed Churches now entertain more reasonable and more scriptural views on those doctrines which were *formerly* the subjects of controversy, what necessity is there of a continued separation?" p. 81.

ORGANIZATION OF THE GENERAL SYNOD AT HAGERSTOWN IN 1820.

After successive Synods and committees of both sides, had failed to make a satisfactory progress towards the desired union of the Lutheran and German Reformed Churches, the subject was dismissed; and soon after, the project of forming *a general union between all the different Evangelical Lutheran Synods of our land,* engaged the attention of the most enlightened and active ministers and members of our Church. In 1819 the Rev. G. Shober, of Salem, North Carolina, appeared at the meeting of the Synod of Pennsylvania and the neighboring States, then convened in Baltimore, and invited the attention of that body to the formation of a general union of all the Evangelical Lutheran Synods then existing in our country. He brought with him a draft of a constitution, bearing strong affinity to that of the General Assembly of the Presbyterian Church. There was, however, no disposition in our Churches generally, and especially in the Synods of New York and Pennsylvania, to form a union of so close a nature, or to invest the General Synod with so much power. That draft was therefore referred to a committee, including the Rev. Shober, who reported a more liberal plan of union, known as the *Plan-Entwurf*, or Sketch of a plan, which was adopted by the Synod as the basis of the constitution for the General Synod, formed at Hagerstown in 1820. But this constitution still was less stringent than the sketch adopted by the Synod at Baltimore. The latter proposed to give to the General Synod the exclusive power to introduce new books for general use in public worship, as well as the right to make alterations in the existing Liturgy: whereas the constitution, as actually adopted at Hagerstown, gave not only to the General Synod, but also to every District Synod, the right of proposing books and writings for public use in the churches, such as catechisms, forms of liturgy, collections of hymns, or "*Confessions of Faith*," after having first submitted a copy thereof to the General Synod, to "receive their advice thereon," which advice had no other than suasive force. This constitution, with some alterations, has been the organic law of the General Synod till the present time.

As the sections of the original constitution above referred to have been altered, and are at present accessible to few even of our ministers, we here introduce them:—

Extract from the Sketch of a proposed Plan for Central Union of the Evangelical Lutheran Church, adopted at Baltimore in 1819. p. 5.

§ 4. "The General Synod possesses the exclusive right, with the consent of a majority of the District Synods, not only to introduce new books for general public use in the churches, but also to make improvements in the Liturgy. But until this is done, the hymn-books, or collections of hymns, now in use, the Smaller Catechism of Luther, the adopted Liturgies, and such other books as have been received as Church books by the existing Synods, shall remain in public use at the option of said Synods. But the General Synod has no power to make or demand any change whatever in the doctrines *which have hitherto been received amongst us.*"

Constitution of the General Synod, as actually adopted at Hagerstown in 1820; p. 7, Art. III. § 2 of the original copy:—

"With regard to all *Books and Writings* proposed for common and public use in the Church, the General Synod shall act as a joint committee of the special Synods and Ministeriums, after the following manner, viz.:—

"1. The General Synod shall examine all books and writings, such as *catechisms*, *forms of liturgy*, collections of hymns or *confessions of faith*, proposed by the *special* District Synods for public use, and give their well-considered advice, counsel or opinion concerning the same. No Synod, therefore, and no Ministerium, standing in connection with this General Synod, shall set forth any new book or writing, of the kind above mentioned, for public use in the Church, without having previously transmitted a full and complete copy thereof to the General Synod, for the purpose of receiving their said advice, counsel or opinion.

"2. Whenever the General Synod shall deem it proper or necessary, they may propose to the Special Synods or Ministeriums new books or writings, *of the kind mentioned above*, for general or special, common or public use. Every proposal of the kind the several or respective Synods and Ministeriums shall duly consider, and if they, or any of them, shall be of opinion, that the said book or books, writing or writings, will not conduce to the end proposed, then and in such a case it is hoped that the reasons of such opinion will be transmitted to the next convention of the General Synod, in order that the same may be entered on their Journal.

"3. But no General Synod can be allowed to possess or arrogate to itself the power of *prescribing* among us uniform *ceremonies of religion* for every part of the Church, or to introduce *such alterations* in matters appertaining to the faith, or to the mode of publishing the gospel of Jesus Christ,—the Son of God and ground of our faith and hope,—*as might, in any way, tend to burden the consciences of the brethren in Christ.*"

After the Pennsylvania Synod had attended one meeting of the General Synod, at Frederick, in 1821, they withdrew from the body in the Spring of 1823, in consequence of a popular clamor in some of their congregations against the General Synod, and Theological Seminaries, Bible Societies, Tract Societies, &c. having been led by some renegades from Germany, and some political demagogues in their midst, to suspect these institutions and associations of being parts of a secret scheme to unite Church and State in this country.* For thirty years after this the Pennsylvania Synod stood aloof from the General Synod. Some were hostile to the decidedly evangelical principles developed and practices encouraged by that body, such as prayer-meetings, protracted meetings, &c., whilst a few ministers and many of their members sympathized with us, and

* For more specific details, see the writer's History of the American Lutheran Church, p. 223, &c.

even contributed to our several religious enterprises, such as the Theological Seminary of the General Synod. Some were also displeased at our early recognition of the Augsburg Confession, for the Pennsylvania Synod had not pledged its members to any other symbol but the Bible for twenty years before, and as long after the organization of the General Synod.

During the last fifteen years, the Pennsylvania Synod has been gradually returning to the peculiarities of the symbolic system of the 16th century, withdrawing more and more from the spirit of Christian fellowship with the Church of Christ in general, and strengthening the framework of her own denominational organization.* The fathers of

* How different the spirit which actuated our fathers, may be seen in their co-operation, not only with the Swedish Lutherans and Episcopalians, but also on proper occasions with ministers of all denominations. At the retirement of General Washington from the Presidential chair, on the 4th of March, 1797, we find those venerable men, Drs. Helmuth and Schmidt, and Dr. Collin, of the Swedish Church, uniting with ministers of the Episcopal, Presbyterian, German Reformed, and several other denominations, in a congratulatory address to him who, under God, was the most distinguished instrument in the establishment of our republic. As that document is rarely met with, our readers will be gratified to see it. To us as Lutherans, it possesses special and permanent value as a memorial of the liberality, the loyalty, and public spirit of our fathers. See Appendix No. III.

the General Synod sought to promote the unity of Christ's body; but the Pennsylvania Synod, together with the different symbolic German, Swedish and Norwegian Synods, confine all their labors, and mainly their aspirations also, to the building up of the wall of partition between them and other portions of Christ's kingdom. Since the return of the Pennsylvania Synod, in 1853, to the General Synod, she has created incessant discord in that body, as also in the Theological Seminary at Gettysburg, by her constant scheming to change the doctrinal basis of both institutions. In 1864, her delegates withdrew from the General Synod, on account of the reception of the Frankean Synod into that body. In 1866, the separation was completed; and hereafter, both institutions will be free from such annoyance, will consist of homogeneous elements, and we trust will live in peace with each other.

On all the points of difference between us and the more rigidly symbolic Synods of our Church, both foreign and native, including some of our most esteemed friends, it is the object of this little volume to show, that the positions of the General Synod are more enlightened and more scriptural than those of our opponents, and exhibit a decidedly higher and more expansive phase of Christianity,—a Christianity whose "field is the world," and whose controlling principle is the declaration of the Saviour: "One is your Master, Christ, and ye are all brethren." In doing this, it will also be apparent, that our Churches afford greater facilities for the conversion of sinners, and for the sanctification and salvation of professed followers of the Lamb. This is effected by the superior prominence given to *individual personal religion*, and to the individual spiritual culture of church-members, as well as by the stronger line of demarcation drawn by our system between the Church and the world.

CHAPTER VII.

On Church Development.

ECCLESIASTICAL development, in its strictest sense, is that series of changes in the doctrines, government, discipline and worship of the Church, which naturally and legitimately flows from the principles of Christianity in the course of its history, as it is affected by the progress of universal science, and the political and social institutions of men.

But this definition, though often adopted, would be correct only, if all Christians had proved faithful to the teachings of the Divine Word; for it ignores those changes which were violations of them, and therefore detrimental to the Church.

It is, moreover, incorrect, as frequently understood, since it virtually denies the freedom of the human will, and supposes all the changes, good and evil, to flow from a necessity arising from the intrinsic nature of their antecedents.

We, therefore, adopt a more comprehensive definition, and by ecclesiastical development understand those changes, for better or worse, in the doctrines, government, discipline and worship, which have been made by the Church in the course of her history, and under the superintendence of Divine Providence, by a correct or incorrect application of the principles and precepts of primitive Christianity in its contact with the political, civil, and social institutions of men, and with the progressive improvements of universal science.

The theories of development are the several philosophical hypotheses, or supposed principles, by which men have endeavored to trace these changes to their causes, thus attempting to determine their relation as either that of causation or mere antecedence and consequence.

God, as a being of infinite wisdom, would necessarily have some design or end in view, in the exercise of his creative energies, in the formation of the myriads of worlds which occupy the regions of space. Equally evident is it, that, having created this wonderful system of worlds, he would also govern them for the attainment of his contemplated end. The general and uniform changes in physical nature, it is conceded, he effects by the exercise of his divine omnipotence, and is therefore himself their efficient cause. The actions of irrational creatures he regulates by periodical appetites, by instincts and some traces of intellect, not amounting to responsibility. But of the *voluntary* actions of his moral agent, man, God could not consistently determine to be the efficient cause himself. Having resolved to create a multitude of free agents, he determines everything efficiently relating to their physical and intellectual nature, and the time, place and other circumstances of their existence. But their *voluntary* actions he influences only by his word, which prescribes the end of their being and the path of their duty, under all circumstances, as well as by his providence and spirit. If, in defiance of this suasive moral influence, man resolves to violate the divine law, and to frustrate the end of his being, God could easily prevent the execution of his purpose by the paralysis of his physical and intellectual powers, or by touching him with the hand of death. Hence, if he permits him to execute his sinful purpose, it is because he can overrule his crimes for the good of others, or of the sinner himself, or for the promotion of his own glory, by the exercise of his punitive justice.

With these principles in view, how shall we account for the changes which have occurred in the Church through the lapse of centuries? What theory do the Scriptures and the facts of history sustain? Is the holy God their author, or is it fallible man?

Or, are there really no moral, or free, or responsible agents in the world? Is there no difference between mind and matter, virtue and vice? Is the universe, including God himself, but one substance, and do all things occur by fixed, unchangeable laws, thus justifying the infidel maxim, "*Whatever is, is right*"? The dictate of common sense, which, though not elaborated into a theory until in later ages, has been, that two factors must be admitted; that as these changes belong to the moral agency of man, they should be attributed either to their fidelity to God's Word, or to the want of it, under the various circumstances of their situation, and under the *overruling providential guidance* of the Great Head of the Church. Hence, every development in accordance with God's Word, is regarded as an improvement in the Church; and the glory is ascribed to God, by whose grace his children, such as the Reformers, were enabled to accomplish it; whilst every change opposed to the inspired Word, we regard as the agency of sinful man, as a corruption of the truth as it is in Jesus.

But of late, theories of more or less infidel tendency have been broached, representing all the actions of men as necessary and as unavoidable, and the volitions of the mind no less so than the circulation of the blood. In short, this theory regards the entire progress of history as a process of nature, developing itself according to eternal, unchangeable laws, in which human actions and reactions are interwoven as involuntary constituents.* And the celebrated Puseyite, and Romish pervert from the Episcopal Church, Mr. J. Henry Newman, maintains, that the increase or expansion of the Christian creed and ritual, together with the variations attending the process in individual writers, are the necessary attendants on any system of philosophy occupying the mind of man, and developed by contact with various influences.†

When we examine the Word of God, our only infallible guide, we find it fully confirming *the theory of common sense.* We find some things concerning the doctrines, the organization, and forms of worship of the Church definitely fixed, and others left undecided, and referred to the judgment of the Church herself in all ages.

Thus, I. the *fundamental doctrines*, which all the so-called Evangelical denominations agree in finding in Scripture, must be regarded as fixed and unalterable in all their essential features, whilst other topics are named in the sacred volume, on which its instructions are not so clear as to have produced uniformity in the Church, and these are proper topics for further investigation

* See Dr. Herzog's Encyclopedia Theol., vol vii. p. 626.

† See Modern Atheism, by Dr. Buchanan, p. 117.

and development. The most authentic list of fundamental doctrines ever made out by the Christian Church is that prepared by the *Evangelical Alliance* convened in London in 1846. That body, consisting of about 1000 of the most distinguished men of all Evangelical denominations in the world, after mature deliberation and most able discussion, pronounced the following doctrines to be fundamental, viz.:—1. The divine inspiration, authority and sufficiency of the Holy Scriptures. 2. The right and duty of private judgment in the interpretation of the Scriptures. 3. The unity of the Godhead, and the Trinity of persons therein. 4. The utter depravity of human nature, in consequence of the fall. 5. The incarnation of the Son of God,—his work of atonement for sinners of mankind,—and his mediatorial intercession and reign. 6. The justification of the sinner by faith alone. 7. The work of the Holy Spirit in the conversion and sanctification of the sinner. 8. The divine institution of the Christian ministry, and the obligation and perpetuity of Baptism and the Lord's Supper. 9. The immortality of the soul. 10. The judgment of the world by our Lord Jesus Christ, with the eternal blessedness of the righteous, and eternal punishment of the wicked. These doctrines, in their essential features as stated, are unchangeable, and always to be adhered to.

II. In regard to the *Mode of Worship.*—Its several parts are enumerated, namely, the preaching and reading of the Word, prayer, singing, and the Sacraments, or the positive institutions of the Church, Baptism and the Lord's Supper, and these must ever remain. But the circumstances attending this worship, the mode of performing it, liturgy or no liturgy, extemporaneous or prescribed prayers, written or unwritten sermons, their length and frequency, the kind of music in singing, vocal alone, or with instrumental accompaniment, &c., — all these and other circumstances are left to the discretion and development of the Church in every age.

III. The form of *Government and Discipline* is fixed as to *essentials;* but many points are undecided. The office of elder, or bishop, or pastor, or steward, — which terms are all used synonymously in Scripture, to signify the ordinary preacher, — was fixed. The power of government and discipline was ultimately vested in the church-members. And that deacons were appointed for *lay* duties, to assist "at tables," and distribute the contributions of the faithful to the poor, is certain; whether, as others contend, they also preached, and constituted a separate and lower order of the ministry, as Episcopalians affirm, and Lutherans as well as Presbyterians deny, is a point for investigation. The primitive Churches also were independent, each being in itself a complete Church of Christ; and there was one (*pro re nata*) council held at Jerusalem, *Acts XV.* Whether the principle of mutual consultation should be frequently recurred to, and how often; or whether it may be systematized into regular annual Synods, and even a General Synod, or Assembly, are subjects of expediency, and left to the decision of the Church in every age, that is, to the development of the Church. It is evident then—

I. That the field of lawful church development embraces those points of Christian doctrine, duty, church government, and public worship, which are less clearly revealed in God's Word, so that the several evangelical denominations differ in regard to them.

II. The *progress of universal science* will necessarily require some change of views and practice on those points, in which they stand related to different parts of Christian doctrine, duty, or mode of worship.

1. Thus, the progress of sacred *philology*, *exegesis*, and *archeology*, will continue to throw increasing light on some portions of Scripture; making them more intelligible to the learned through the originals, and to the populace by means of commentaries and improved translations. The fixed opposition to all, even the most judicious propositions to amend the common English version of Scripture, even after

the acknowledged progress of sacred science, in the last several centuries, seems to be unwise and prejudicial to the interests of the truth.

2. As *popular education and intelligence* become more generally diffused, the exercises of the pulpit will necessarily be elevated as to the grade of literary and theological excellence, in order to retain their influence over the hearers.

3. The progress of improvement in the *science of music*, will naturally improve the mode of singing, and thus affect this portion of the public worship. Yet the utmost caution should be observed that this exercise be not conducted in so complicated a manner as to be above the capacity of the congregation, and to cause the church to approximate the character of a theatre, whither ungodly lovers of music resort, to be entertained by the scientific and highly artistic performances of the choir and organ, but in which the congregation generally can neither join nor find edification. This unscriptural development may be justly charged on the Romish Church; but are there not some Protestant Churches which are evidently tending in the same direction? In short, the whole question of introducing instrumental music, and especially the organ, into New Testament churches, is a very solemn one, and by no means to be considered as decided. Certain it is, that congregations having revivals are strongly

inclined to let the organ remain silent on such occasions, under the impression that its obviously *mechanical* nature and constant interruptions by interludes, tend to prevent the growth of that profound devotional feeling in the Church, which always accompanies such seasons of deep religious interest.*

What then is the proper attitude for the Church to maintain in regard to any proposed change or development? What are the rules which should direct her conduct?

RULE I. In every proposed change, *we should adhere strictly to the Protestant maxim, that the Bible is the only infallible rule of faith and practice,* and, therefore, also our norm in all attempts at Church development. This is the grand principle, adopted by *Luther and the leading Reformers* of the 16th century, which enabled them to throw off the great mass of Romish errors and superstitions. This rule has been so frequently and fully discussed by Protestant writers of all denominations, that we need add nothing more on this occasion. It is applicable to everything relating to doctrine, government, discipline, and worship, at any time introduced into the Church of God.

RULE II. In all proposed amendments, which

* See the author's discussion of this subject in the Appendix to his Sermon on Spiritual Worship, Appendix, 2d edition.

may seem to be called for by *improvements* in any department of *universal science,* or in the *habits or views of society,* the following questions should be asked in reference to each contemplated change: 1. Is it accordant with the declarations of God's Word, bearing on the subject? 2. Is it agreeable to the general principles laid down by Scripture on similar subjects? 3. Does it harmonize with the *general design* of Scripture, and of the Church? 4. Is it favorable to personal religion, and promotive of the progress of Christ's kingdom? If these questions can be correctly answered in the affirmative, then the development is a legitimate one, is pleasing to the great Head of the Church, and will promote his kingdom. But in all other cases, the change will be for the worse, and the development not be accordant with our obligations. Nor let it ever be forgotten, that whilst Christians endeavor faithfully to do their duty, the Head of the Church presides over her destinies, and guides the course of her history by providential influences, physical, intellectual and moral, and "dwells with his people alway to the end of the world."

REFORMATORY DEVELOPMENT.

Church development may be regarded as *retrospective* or reformatory, as well as prospective. On the principles above stated, and the rules appended to them, the Reformers conducted and effected the great REFORMATION of the 16th century. Their work consisted in a return toward the apostolic purity of the Church. Without entering further into particulars, the Lutheran Reformers by legitimate development rejected the following errors of doctrine and practice:

The Papacy and Papal Hierarchy. See Smalcald Art. IV.

Transsubstantiation. See Augsburg Conf., Art. X.

The necessity of enumerating all individual sins in Private Confession. Aug. Conf., Art. XI.

Justification by Works. Aug. Conf., Art. IV.

Invocation of Saints. Aug. Conf., Art. XXI.

Celibacy of the Priesthood. Augsburg Conf., Art. XXIII.

Withholding the cup from the laity in the Eucharist. Augsburg Conf., Art. XXII.

The Mass. Augs. Conf., Art. XXIV.

Diversity of Meats. Augs. Conf., Art. XXVI.

Monastic Vows. Augs. Conf., Art. XXVII.

The usurped power of the Bishops and Priests. Augs. Conf., Art. XXVIII.

Purgatory. Smalcald Art. II.

These are the prominent points which distinguish the Protestant from the Romish Church. They are changes in the state of the Romanism as it existed before the Reformation, developments in accordance with the Word of God, and the other principles of development above described.

After the lapse of three centuries, these errors are still rejected by the Lutheran Church, in all parts of the world, where her ministrations are found.

During the lapse of these centuries, various vicissitudes have attended our Church in Europe, and various changes or developments have occurred, some for better and others for worse. The Lutheran Church in this country has more or less sympathized with the changes experienced by the mother Church in the Old World. But the Church having been entirely divorced from the civil government in this country, she has enjoyed more unrestricted opportunity for scriptural and legitimate development, by the rejection of the few remaining errors contained in the former symbols of the 16th century, and by the adjustment of her framework to the progress of truth and science, as well as to the approaching latter-day glory of her Lord.

These several points of development are comparatively of minor moment, and the errors repudiated have been rejected by many ministers, who are not connected with the General Synod. Some isolated Synods also have experienced a salutary development by excluding from binding authority the entire collection of the former symbolical books, except the Augsburg Confession, whilst they rigidly adhere to all its contents.

The General Synod, at her organization in 1820, acknowledged the binding authority of no symbol beyond the Bible; but five years afterwards, desiring to bear public testimony to the truth in Jesus, as understood by her, she avowed the additional position that *the fundamental doctrines of the Bible are taught in the doctrinal articles of the Augsburg Confession.** In 1866 the General Synod extended this same qualified obligation to the remaining seven articles, which discuss the Romish errors or abuses, rejected by the Confessors.

The remaining errors retained in the Augsburg Confession, but denied by nearly all the ministers of the General Synod, are:—

1. *The clause approving* of what are termed "*The Ceremonies of the Mass.*" These ceremonies are, in fact, now rejected by all Lutheran Churches, so far as they had specific reference to the Mass proper. For the correct understanding of that phrase, it may be proper to remark, that the word "mass," in the literature of the Reformation, was also *sometimes* used to designate the Lord's Supper. Further, that

* This language was contained in the Statutes prepared and reported to the Synod by the present writer, as the basis of her intended Theological Seminary, in 1825, subsequently located at Gettysburg.

there were *no special ceremonies preceding the Lord's Supper*, other than those called "ceremonies of the mass;" which amount to about an hour's reading of prayers and gospels, of genuflexions and *elevation of the host*, crossings, tergiversations, &c. These were the ceremonies preceding the Mass proper, performed by the priest alone, for the benefit *of others;* and the Lord's Supper, or Communion, as it was called, followed *immediately after, without any other introductory ceremonies.* Hence, practically and really, this same set of ceremonies belonged both to *the* Mass and the Lord's Supper; and passages can be found, in some of which the ceremonies appear to be predicated of the Mass proper, and in others of the Eucharist. The word "mass," therefore, has several meanings, sometimes signifying the Mass proper, at others the Lord's Supper, and at others the entire service including both, and perhaps sometimes the ceremonies of the Mass without the self-communion of the priest. Thus, also, the phrase "going to preaching," signifies going to attend *worship* in general; yet, at others, the word "preaching" signifies *specifically* the sermon. This error is taught in the following passages of the *Augsburg Confession*, Art. 24, or Topic 3 of The Abuses Corrected:—

CEREMONIES OF THE MASS.

"It is unjustly charged against our Churches, that they have abolished the Mass. For it is notorious that the Mass is celebrated among us with greater devotion and seriousness than by our opponents. Our people are also instructed repeatedly, and with the utmost diligence, concerning the design and proper mode of receiving the holy sacrament; namely, to comfort alarmed consciences, by which means the people are attracted to the Communion *and the Mass.* We at the same time give instruction against other erroneous doctrines concerning the Sacrament. In the public ceremonies of the Mass, also, no other perceptible change has been made than that at several places German hymns are sung along with the Latin, in order to instruct and exercise the people; since all ceremonies are chiefly designed to teach the people what it is necessary for them to know concerning Christ."—*Translated in Lutheran Manual of the present writer*, pp. 287, 288.

Apology to the Augsburg Confession, Art. XII.

"*In the first place*, we must mention, by way of introduction, that we do not abolish the Mass; for Mass is held in our churches on every Sunday and festival, when the Sacrament is administered to those who desire it, but only after they have been examined and absolved. Besides, Christian ceremonies are likewise observed, in reading, singing, praying," &c.—p. 310, *Newmarket 2d Edition of the Symbolic Books.*

"We have shown in our Confession, that we hold that the Eucharist or the Mass does not confer grace, *ex opere operato,* and that Mass, performed for others, does not merit for them the remission of sins, of punishment, and guilt. And for this position, we have the strong and indubitable grounds, that it is impossible for us to obtain the forgiveness of sin through our works, *ex opere operato,*—that is, through the performed work in itself, *sine bono motu utentis,* without regard to the disposition of the mind, or though there be no good emotion in the heart."—*Idem,* p. 312.

2. *The second error rejected is, Private Confession and Absolution.* The necessity of enumerating all our particular sins to the priest at confession, termed *Auricular Confession,* Luther and his adherents rejected; but *Private Confession,* at which the individual confessed his sinfulness and penitence in general, together with *absolution,* was long retained in the Lutheran Church of Germany, although rejected from the beginning in Sweden and Denmark where nothing more than a public confession of the congregation together, before Communion, was retained.

"Absolution was received *privately*, by each one, *individually*, *kneeling* before the *confessional*, the confessor *imposing his hands* at the time. Private confession was given *only in the church*, in which the confessional was so located *near the pulpit*, that *no other person could be near, or hear* what was said by the penitent."—*Funk's Kirchenordnungen*, &c., pp. 189, 190.

As the Sacred Volume contains not a single command that laymen should confess their sins to ministers, any more than ministers to laymen; and as not a single such example of confession and absolution is contained in the Word of God, our American Church has universally repudiated the practice. By the old Lutheran Synod of Missouri, consisting entirely of Europeans, this rite is still observed.

We therefore reject the following passages:

OF PRIVATE CONFESSION.

Augsburg Confession, Art. XI.

"In reference to Confession it is taught, that Private Absolution ought to be retained in the Church, and should not be discontinued. In Confession, however, it is unnecessary to enumerate all transgressions and sins, which indeed is not possible. *Psalm* xix. 12: 'Who can understand his errors?'"

Augsburg Confession, Art. XXV.

"Confession is not abolished by our ministers. For the custom is retained among us, not to administer the Sacrament unto those who have not been previously examined and absolved. The people, moreover, are diligently instructed with regard to the comfort afforded by the words of absolution, and the high and great estimation in which it is to be held; for it is not the voice or word of the individual present, but it is the word of God who here forgives sins; for it is spoken in God's stead, and by his command. Concerning this command and power of the keys, it is taught with the greatest assiduity how comfortable, how useful they are to alarmed consciences, and besides how God requires confidence in this absolution, no less than if the voice of God was heard from heaven; and by this we comfort ourselves, and know that through such faith we obtain the remission of sins."

Augsburg Confession, Art. XXVIII.

"Accordingly they teach, that the power of the keys or of the bishops, according to the Gospel, is a power and commission from God to preach the Gospel, *to remit and to retain sins*."—p. 134.

How dangerous the entire doctrine of absolution and sin-forgiving power of the ministry is, to the spirituality of the Church, and to the doctrine of justification by grace alone through faith in Jesus Christ, is clearly evident.

The Scriptures, and also the Reformers, teach that pardon or justification can be obtained only through the merits of Christ, which merits must be apprehended by a living faith, which living faith can be found only in the regenerate or converted soul. Hence, as none but a regenerate sinner can exercise living faith, no other can be pardoned, whatever else he may do or possess. Now, those who attend Confession are either regenerate, or they are not. If they were regenerated or converted before they went to Confession, they had faith, and were pardoned before; if they were unregenerate or unconverted, then neither their confession nor the priest's absolution can confer pardon on them, because they have not a living faith, although they may be sincere and exercise some sorrow for their sins. On the other hand, if any amount of seriousness and penitence, short of true conversion or regeneration, could, through the Confessional, or any other rite, confer pardon of sin, the line of distinction between converted and unconverted, between mere formalists and true Christians, would be obliterated; we should have pardoned saints and pardoned sinners in the Church, converted and unconverted heirs of the promise, believing and unbelieving subjects of justification, and the words of the Lord Jesus would prove a lie, "That *unless a man be born again, he cannot enter the kingdom of heaven.*"

As to the passage, *Matth.* xviii. 18, "Whatsoever ye shall bind on earth shall be bound in heaven; and whatsoever ye shall loose on earth shall be loosed in heaven;" it evidently refers to acts of church discipline, such as "telling it to the church," &c., which are expressly mentioned in the previous part of the passage. And that in *John* xx. 23, "Whosesoever sins ye remit, they are remitted unto them; and whosesoever sins ye retain, they are retained," was uttered on a different occasion, after the Saviour's resurrection, and either refers to a miraculous power bestowed on the apostles to discern the condition of the heart, and to announce pardon of God to truly penitent individuals; or it confers on the ministry, in all ages, the power to announce *in general* the conditions on which God will pardon sinners; but it contains no authority for applying these promises to individuals, as is done in private absolution.

3. *The third error rejected is the denial of the Divine institution and obligation of the Christian Sabbath or Lord's Day.*—Our American Churches believe in the Divine institution and obligation of the Christian Sabbath or Lord's Day, convinced that

the Old Testament Sabbath was not a mere Jewish institution, but that it was appointed by God at the close of the creative week, when he rested on the seventh day, and blessed it, and sanctified it, (*Gen.* ii. 2, 3,) that is, set it apart for holy purposes, for reasons of universal and perpetual nature, (*Exod.* xx. 11.) Even in the re-enactment of it in the Mosaic code, its original appointment is acknowledged: "*Remember* the Sabbath-Day,—because in six days God made heaven and earth, and rested on the *seventh; wherefore* he (*then*, in the beginning) *blessed the Sabbath-Day, and hallowed it.*" Now this reason has no more reference to the Jews than to any other nation, and if it was sufficient to make the observance of the Sabbath obligatory on them, it must be equally so for all other nations before and after them.

Since, therefore, the observance and sanctification of a portion of his time is based on universal reasons in the nature of man, especially as a religious being, and the proportion of time was fixed at a *seventh* by the example and precepts of the Creator in the beginning, the Sabbath must be universally obligatory, and the abrogation of the Mosaic ritual can at most only repeal those ceremonial additions which that ritual made, and must leave the original Sabbath as it found it. Now, whilst the apostles and first Christians, under the inspired guidance, for a season also attended worship on the Jewish Sabbath, yet they observed the day of the Lord's resurrection—the first day of the week—as their day of special religious convocations; and this inspired example is obligatory on Christians in all ages. Still, the essence of the institution consists, not in the particular day of the week, though that is now fixed, but in the religious observance of one day in seven.

We therefore reject the doctrine taught in the former symbolical books, in which the Sabbath is treated as a mere Jewish institution, and supposed to be totally revoked; whilst the propriety of retaining the Lord's Day as a day of religious worship is supposed to rest only on the agreement of the Churches for the convenience of general convocation. Hence we reject the following passages:

Augsburg Confession, Art. XXVIII.

"And what are we to believe concerning *Sunday*, (the Lord's Day,) and other similar ordinances and ceremonies of the Church? To this inquiry we reply, the bishops and clergy may make regulations, that order may be observed in the church, not with the view of thereby obtaining the grace of God, nor in order thus to make satisfaction for sins, nor to bind the consciences to hold and regard this as a necessary worship of God, or to believe that they would commit sin if they violated these regulations without offence to others. Thus St. Paul to the Corinthians (1 *Cor.* xi. 5) has ordained that women shall have their heads covered in the congregation; also, that ministers should not all speak at the same time in the congregation, but in an orderly manner, one after another.

"It is becoming in a Christian congregation to observe such order, for the sake of love and peace, and to obey the bishops and clergy in these cases, and to observe these regulations so far as not to give offence to one another, so that there may be no disorder or unbecoming conduct in the Church. Nevertheless, the consciences of men must not be oppressed, by representing these things as necessary to salvation, or teaching that they are guilty of sin, if they break these regulations without offence to others; for no one affirms that a woman commits sin who goes out with her head uncovered, without giving offence to the people. Such, also, is the ordinance concerning Sunday, Easter, Whitsunday, and similar festivals and customs. For those who suppose that the ordinance concerning Sunday instead of Sabbath is enacted as necessary are greatly mistaken. For the Holy Scripture has abolished the Sabbath, and teaches that all the ceremonies of the old law may be omitted, since the publication of the Gospel. And yet, as it was necessary to appoint a certain day, in order that the people might know when they should assemble, the Christian Church has appointed Sunday (the Lord's Day) for this purpose; and to this change she was the more inclined and willing, that the people might have an example of Christian liberty, and might know that the observance of neither the Sabbath nor any other day is necessary. There have been numerous erroneous disputations published, concerning the change of the law, the ceremonies of the New Testament, and the change of the Sabbath, which have all sprung from the false and erroneous opinion, that Christians must have such a mode of Divine worship as is conformed to the Levitical or Jewish service, and that Christ enjoined it on the apostles and bishops to invent new ceremonies, which should be necessary to salvation."—*See the Lutheran Manual*, pp. 306, 307.

4. *The fourth error rejected is that of Baptismal Regeneration.*—By this designation is meant the doctrine that baptism is necessarily and invariably attended by spiritual regeneration, and that such water baptism is unconditionally essential to salvation.

In the case of all adults, the Scriptures represent *faith in Christ* as the necessary prerequisite to baptism, and baptism as a rite by which those who had already consecrated themselves to Christ, or been converted, made a public profession of the fact, received a pledge of the Divine favor, or of forgiveness of sins, and were admitted to membership in the visible Church. The same inspired records also teach, that if men are destitute of this faith, if they believe not, they shall be damned, notwithstanding their baptism. "He that *believeth* and is baptized shall be saved, and he that *believeth* not shall be damned," *Matt.* xvi. 16. And Philip said to the eunuch, "If thou *believest* with all thy heart thou mayest be baptized," *Acts* viii. 37. "*Repent* and be baptized," *Acts* ii. 38; viii. 62; xviii. 8. Hence, if baptism required previous faith and repentance or conversion in adults, and if, when they were destitute of this faith or conversion, they were damned notwithstanding their baptism, it follows that baptism was not, and is not, a converting ordinance in adults, and does not necessarily effect or secure their regeneration.

Now that baptism cannot accomplish more in infants than in adults is self-evident; hence, if it is not a converting ordinance in adults, it cannot be in infants.

Baptism in *adults* is a means of making a public profession of previous faith, or of being received into the visible Church, as well as a pledge and condition of obtaining those blessings purchased by Christ, and offered to all who repent, believe in him, and profess his name by baptism.

Baptism, in *infants*, is the pledge of the bestowment of those blessings purchased by Christ for all. "As in Adam all die, even so in Christ shall all be made alive." And "The promise is to you and your *children*," *Acts* ii. 39. These blessings are forgiveness of sins, or exemption from the penal consequences of natural depravity, (which would at least be exclusion from heaven on account of moral disqualification for admission,) reception into the visible Church of Christ, grace to help in every time of need, and special provision for the nurture and admonition in the Lord, to which parents pledge themselves.

The language of the Saviour to Nicodemus, *John* iii. 6, "*Unless a man be born of water and the Spirit*," probably refers also to baptism, which had been known to the Jews, and practised by John the Baptist, before the ministry of Christ, as a mode of *public reception* of proselytes, who were then said to be new-born. Its import is to inform Nicodemus that he must *publicly* profess the religion of Jesus by baptism, and also be regenerated by the Holy Spirit, if he desired to enter the kingdom of Heaven. Thus also the words, *Acts* xxii. 16, "*Arise and be baptized, and wash away thy sins*," were addressed to Paul *after* he had surrendered himself to Christ, and signifies: "Arise, and publicly profess Christ by baptism, and thus complete your dedication of yourself to his cause, the condition on the sincere performance of which God will, for Christ's sake, pardon your sins.

Baptismal regeneration, either in infants or adults, is therefore a doctrine not taught in the Word of God, and fraught with much injury to the souls of men, although inculcated in the former symbolical books. At the same time, whilst the doctrine of baptismal regeneration certainly did prevail in our European Churches, it is proper to remark that the greater part of the passages in the former symbols relating to this subject are (and doubtless may be) explained by many to signify no more than we above inculcate.

BAPTISMAL REGENERATION.

Augsburg Confession, Art. II.

"Our Churches teach that this innate disease and original sin is truly sin, and condemneth all those under the eternal wrath of God who are not *born again by Baptism and the Holy Spirit.*"

How this article was understood is seen from the following passages:

Apology to Augsburg Confession, p. 226.

"Our opponents also agree to the ninth article, in which we confess that baptism is necessary to salvation, and that the baptism of infants is not fruitless, but necessary and salutary."

Luther's Smaller Catechism.

"*What does Baptism confer or benefit?*

"*Ans.* It effects the forgiveness of sins, delivers from death and the devil, and confers everlasting salvation upon all who believe it, as the words and promises of God declare.

"*How can water effect such great things?*

"*Ans.* Indeed it is not the water that has such effect, but the word of God that is with and in the water, and the faith trusting such word of God in the water. For without the word of God the water is mere water, hence no baptism; but with the word of God it constitutes a baptism—that is, a gracious water of life, and a washing of regeneration, in the Holy Ghost."—*Symb. B.*, p. 421.

Luther's Larger Catechism.

"Every Christian, therefore, has enough to learn and practise in baptism during his life; for he must ever exert himself to maintain a firm faith in what it promises and brings him, namely, triumph over the devil and death, the remission of sins, the grace of God, Christ with all his works, and the Holy Ghost with all his gifts. In short, the blessings of Baptism are so great, that if feeble nature could but comprehend them, we might justly doubt their reality. For, imagine to yourself a physician, who possessed an art preventing persons from dying; or, even if they died, immediately restoring them to life so as to live eternally afterwards; how the world would rush and flock around him with money, while the poor, prevented by the rich, could not approach him! And yet here, in baptism, every one has such a treasure and medicine gratuitously brought to his door—a medicine which abolishes death, and preserves all men to eternal life."—p. 525.

Luther's Larger Catechism.

"It (baptism) is, therefore, very appropriately called food for the soul, which nourishes and strengthens the new man; *for through Baptism we are born anew;* but beside this, the old, vicious nature in the flesh and blood nevertheless adheres to man, in which there are so many impediments and obstacles, with which we are opposed as well by the devil as by the world, so that we often become weary and faint, and sometimes stumble."—*Symb. B.*, p. 533.

In the *Visitation Articles,* published fourteen years after the other Symbolical books for the purpose of explaining their true import, and then made binding in Saxony:—

ART. III.—ON BAPTISM.

§ II. "By baptism as the laver of regeneration, and the renewing of the Holy Ghost, God saves us, and works in us such righteousness and purification from sins, that whosoever perseveres in such covenant and reliance, will not be lost, but have eternal life."

§ IV. "Baptism is the bath (laver) of regeneration, *because in it we are regenerated*, and sealed with the spirit of sonship and obtain pardon."—*Müller's Symb. Bücher*, pp. 848, 849.

5. *The fifth error rejected is the real presence of the body and blood of Christ in the Eucharist.*—The Reformers justly rejected the Romish error, that the bread and wine were transformed and transsubstantiated into the body and blood of Christ. But they still adhered to the opinion, that the real body and blood of the Saviour are present at the Eucharist, in some mysterious way, and are received by the mouth of every communicant, worthy or unworthy.

For this view we find no authority in Scripture. (*a*) On the contrary, when Christ uttered the words: "This (bread) is my body," his body was *not yet dead*, but was reclining at their side at the table; and therefore was certainly not received by them into their mouths. The language was therefore figurative, such as Jesus was wont often to employ.

Thus, "I am the *door*," *John* x. 9. "I am the *true vine*," xv. 1. "The *field* is the *world*," "the *seed* is the Word," &c.

(*b*) Christ himself exhorts us, "Do this in *remembrance* of me:" but remembrance is applicable only to that which is past and absent. Paul also represents the design of this ordinance to be, "To show, or publish, the Lord's death," a *past* event and not a present person. Thus we come into the communion with, or are reminded of, the Lord's body and blood through the emblems of bread and wine.

(*c*) It contradicts the clear and indisputable testimony of our senses, for as the body and blood are to be received by the *mouth* of the communicant, it *must* be a *local* and *material reception*, which, if it did occur at sacramental celebrations, could be observed by the senses.

(*d*) It contradicts the observation of all nations and ages, that every body or material substance must occupy a definite portion of space, and cannot be at more than one place at the same time, and therefore not at a hundred different places where the communion is received simultaneously.

For these and other reasons the great mass of our ministers and churches reject this doctrine, and the annexed passages of the former symbolical books in which it is taught. The disposition to reject this error was manifested by Melanchthon himself, and it prevailed extensively in the latter third of the sixteenth century. But during the first quarter of this century, the conviction that our Reformers did not purge away the whole of the Romish error from this doctrine, gained ground, universally, until the great mass of the whole Lutheran Church, before the year 1817, had rejected the doctrine of the real presence.

REJECTED PASSAGES:

Augsburg Confession, Art. X.

OF THE LORD'S SUPPER.

"Concerning the holy Supper of the Lord, it is taught, that the true body and blood of Christ are truly present, under the form of bread and wine, in the Lord's Supper, and are there administered and received."—*Symb. Books*, p. 112.

The primitive signification of this clause is explained by the other books:

Apology to the Confession, Art. VII., VIII. (IV.)

"Our adversaries (the Romanists) do not object to the tenth article (of the Augsburg Confession), in which we confess that the body and blood of Christ our Lord are truly present in the holy Supper, and administered and received with the visible elements, the bread and wine, as hitherto maintained in the (Romish) Church, and as the Greek Canon shows." —*Symb. Books*, p. 227.

Smalcald, Article VI.

"Concerning the Sacrament of the Altar, we hold that the bread and wine in the Eucharist are the true body and blood of Christ, which are administered and received not only by pious, but also by impious Christians." — *Symb. Books,* p. 384.

Luther's Smaller Catechism.

"*What is the Sacrament of the Altar?*"

"*Ans.* It is the true body and blood of our Lord Jesus Christ, with bread and wine, instituted by Christ himself, for us Christians to eat and to drink." *Symb. Books*, p. 424.

Form of Concord, Pt. I., Art. VII.

"We teach that the true body and blood of our Lord Jesus Christ are truly and essentially, or substantially, present in the Lord's Supper, administered with the bread and wine, and received with the lips, by all those who use this sacrament, be they worthy or unworthy, good or evil, believing or unbelieving; being received by the believing unto consolation and life, but by the unbelieving unto judgment."—*Symb. Books*, p. 570.

"We believe, teach, and confess, that the words

of the Testament of Christ are not to be understood otherwise than according to their literal sense, so that the bread does not signify the absent body of Christ, and the wine the absent blood of Christ, but on account of their sacramental union, *that the bread and wine* ARE *truly the body and blood of Christ.*"—*Idem*, p. 571.

"We believe, teach, and confess, that not only the truly believing and the worthy, but also the unworthy and the unbelieving, receive the true body and blood of Christ."—p. 572.

"In addition to the above clear passages, incontestably teaching the real presence, it deserves to be ever remembered, that only fourteen years after the Form of Concord was published, when Duke Frederick William, during the minority of Christian II., published the VISITATION ARTICLES OF SAXONY, in 1594, in order to suppress the Melanchthonian tendencies to reject this and other peculiarities of the symbols, the Article on this subject which was framed by men confessedly adhering to the old symbols, and designing to re-enunciate their true import, and which was enforced upon the whole Church in Saxony as symbolic, gives the most objectionable view of this doctrine, viz.: I. 'The pure doctrine of our Church is, that the words, '*Take and eat, this is my body: drink, this is my blood*, are to be understood *simply and according to the letter*.' II. That the body (which is received and eaten) is the *proper* and *natural body* (der rechte natürliche Leib) of Christ, *which hung upon the Cross;* and the blood (which is drunk) is the *proper* and *natural blood* (das rechte natürliche Blut) *which flowed from the side of Christ.*' Müller's Symb. Books, p. 847. Now we cannot persuade ourselves, that this is the view of a single minister of the General Synod, or of many out of it; and yet these are the views that those are obligated to receive who avow implicit allegiance to the former symbolical books of our Church in Europe. If any adopt the modification received by many of our distinguished divines, such as Reinhardt and others, they do not faithfully embrace the symbolical doctrine, and cannot fairly profess to do so.

By the rejection of the above remaining errors of the Augsburg Confession, and the restriction of her doctrinal basis to fundamentals, the General Synod may be regarded as having completed her doctrinal development. Her organic structure of Government and Discipline are found in the Formula attached to the Hymn-Book, and her mode of worship is delineated in her Liturgy. The latter two may yet receive further amendment.

It may be proper in this place to add, that at the meeting of the General Synod at York, in 1864, a series of resolutions was passed disclaiming the following errors, so that they have been formally rejected by the General Synod. The last of the series was not duly considered, as the Synod was near its close, and all were desirous of expediting business. It affirms that, rightly interpreted, these errors are not taught in the Augsburg Confession, an assertion contradicted by the practice and professions of a large portion of our European Churches, by our most learned American divines, and by the declarations of the leaders of the Missouri Synod. Yet as we present the appropriate extracts from the Confession, each reader can judge for himself, whether the errors are taught in the quotations or not.

DIFFERENT VIEWS CONCERNING THE PRIMITIVE CHURCH, AS A MODEL FOR ALL FUTURE AGES.

The Church of God on earth may be regarded in a twofold light. There is, first, the body of professors of religion, who constitute the visible church. But the blessed Saviour admonishes us, that, "Not every one that saith unto me, Lord, Lord, shall enter into the kingdom of heaven; but he that doeth the will of my Father who is in heaven." We must, therefore, discriminate between the professed and the real disciples of our Lord; between those who merely exhibit the form of godliness, and those who also possess its power, or, in the language of theology, between the visible and the invisible Church.

The proper organization of the Church of God, in all ages, and especially under the Christian dispensation, is a subject of momentous importance. For that organization is the system of regulations by which the people of God are to be associated together, and directed in working out their salvation with fear and trembling; to serve as depositories of the oracles of God, to watch over each other's spiritual welfare, and, by letting their light shine amongst men, to exert a salutary influence on the world around, thus advancing the kingdom of Christ.* This is the body over which Christ presides, and to which he has promised his presence until the end of the world. When we examine the record of God's dealings with his people through a period of four thousand years, we find the organization of his Church to have been progressive in visibility, progressive in its Christological development, and progressive in its spirituality, as finally interpreted by the Saviour and his inspired apostles. The principal gradations in this development have been termed by theologians the Adamic, the Patriarchal, the Mosaic and the Christian economies, or modes of administration of the Church of God.

* 1 Tim. iii. 15. Eph. iii. 10. Matth. v. 13–16.

As to the last and most perfect stage of this development, found in the New Testament, different views are entertained concerning the degree of conformity to the inspired model, which is required of us. The first is termed *Erastianism,** so called after *Thomas Erastus,* a distinguished physician and theologian of the sixteenth century. He maintained that the Church should exercise no discipline, not even for the grossest immoralities, and should be subjected to the control of the civil magistrates. Thus he denied the autonomy or independence of the Church, and would make it the mere tool of civil rulers. This is one extreme, which, though not fully adopted by the Protestant Churches of Europe, exerted only too much influence upon them. The term Erastianism is, however, also employed with greater latitude, to express the opinion that no form or inspired model of Church government is prescribed in the Scriptures, and that each Church has perfect liberty to adopt such form as she may prefer.

* Thomas Erastus, a physician, and afterwards a Professor of Ethics in the University of Basel, was born September 14th, 1524, probably in the Grand-Duchy of Baden, and died at Basel, December 31st, 1583. He was also Professor of Medicine in the University of Heidelberg, after 1558, and mingled in the theological discussions of the day, in general favoring the views of the Swiss Reformed Church.

The opposite extreme is that of *High-churchism*, whose advocates maintain that *their* system of government, whatever it may be, is taught *in all its essential features in God's Word, and is therefore obligatory on all others.* Hence they gravely venture to unchurch all who differ from them! This view characterizes a large part of the Episcopal Church, both in England and America, known as *High-churchmen.**

The *Golden mean* is that of *Low-churchism*, whose advocates regard the Scriptures as laying down only the essential features and principles for the organization of the Church of Christ, and as wisely leaving all minor arrangements to be settled by each Church according to the peculiar customs and institutions of the country. This adjustment is to have reference to the progressive developments of God's providence and Spirit, as well as to the pro-

* The *High*-church party is at present found almost exclusively in the Episcopal Church of England and America. For many years past the Episcopal Church has been divided on this subject. Of twenty-eight bishops and archbishops in Great Britain, thirteen are classed with the High-church party, five with the Low-church party, and ten occupy an intermediate ground, being sometimes denominated the "Broad Church." The highest shades of High-churchism (says Sawyer) differ but little from Romanism, and the passage is easy from this division of the Church of England to that of Rome.

gressive improvements of mankind in the arts and sciences, which facilitate the progress of Christ's kingdom, such as the art of printing, the steam-press, and international steam communication. To this class belong the several *Low-church* forms of government, the *Independent*, the *Congregational*, the *Presbyterian*, the *Low-church Episcopal*, the *Methodist*, the Lutheran Church generally, and especially the *American Lutheran Churches of the General Synod.*

CHAPTER VIII.

More Immediate and Extended Vindication of the Five Cardinal Features of the General Synod of the American Lutheran Church, as Scriptural Developments of the Church of the Redeemer.

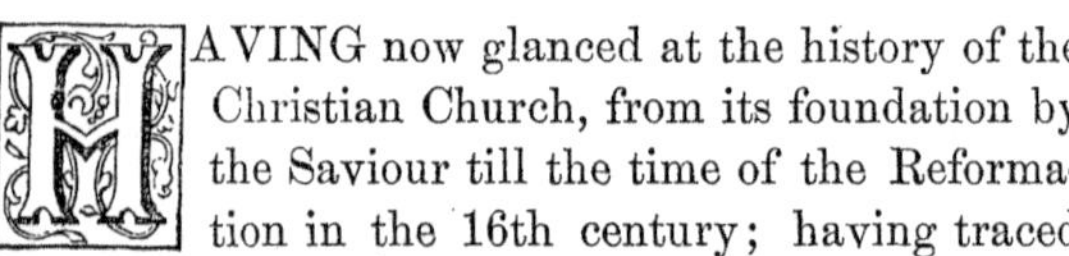

HAVING now glanced at the history of the Christian Church, from its foundation by the Saviour till the time of the Reformation in the 16th century; having traced the Lutheran branch of the Protestant Church from its origin till the establishment of our Church in this country, and the formation of the General Synod; and having discussed the principles of Church development in general, we come to the more immediate and extended demonstration of the position, that in all the cardinal features of its organization, the General Synod of the Evangelical Lutheran Church *is in accordance with the precepts and principles of God's Word.*

I. *First, of the Doctrinal Basis of the General Synod.*—And here some preliminary remarks on the practice of God's people under the old dispensation, and the teachings of the Old and New Testaments on this subject, may not be inappropriate or unacceptable. In the infancy of our race, the theology of the patriarchs embraced but a few cardinal doctrines. These may have been the same which the Jewish Rabbins* term the seven precepts of Noah, said to have been required of the proselytes of the gate, concerning which, however, we know nothing certain, except as far as they are inculcated in God's Word. From the sacred volume we find the following doctrines to have been taught:

The existence and attributes of Jehovah;† the depravity of man;‡ hope of pardon;§ belief of a future state,‖ contrary to the views of Warburton; together with the intimation of a Saviour to come.¶

To *Abraham*, the Father of the Faithful, God revealed the covenant of grace more fully, adding the rite of circumcision to the external organism to the Church.

* See Winer's Biblisches Real-Wörterbuch, Vol. II. p. 285; Jahn's Archæology, § 325, p. 413 (Upham's Version); Buddei, Hist. Eccles. Vel. Test., Vol. I. p. 156.

† Job xxxii. 8. Ps. xix. 1, 2; lxxv. 1.

‡ Gen. vi. 5; viii. 21–8.

§ Gen. iv. 7.

‖ Gen. v. 22–24. Heb. xi. 5. Comp. Gen. v. 22, 24; xxviii. 13; Matt. xxii. 31, 32.

¶ Gen. iii. 15; xii. 3; xvii. 19; xxii. 18; xxvi. 4; xlix. 10.

Under the *Mosaic dispensation* he completed the Old Testament development, both in doctrine and organization; illustrating it progressively by prophecies and types and psalms, and retaining out of the patriarchal religion all the features which his infinite wisdom deemed proper. Such were sacrifices, the priesthood,* circumcision, the distinction of meats, tithes, the moral precepts, and the Sabbath. Especially did he develop the grand doctrine of the Messiah to come. Now all these doctrines are taught in the Old Testament in popular and not in systematic language; so that differences of interpretation might naturally arise. Yet we have no knowledge of the Church's having ever formed a human *creed*, and required its members to assent to it, either orally or by subscription.

NO UNINSPIRED CREED IN THE OLD TESTAMENT CHURCH.

But some may inquire, were there actually any important differences of interpretation in the Old dispensation, such as are now alleged as sufficient reason for introducing uninspired extended creeds into the Church? That such differences of moment did exist among them, their own historian, *Josephus*. abundantly teaches.† Hear also the testimony of

* Numb. iii. 12, 13.

† Josephus' Antiquities of the Jews, B. 18, ch. 1

Jahn, the learned archæologist, on this subject:* "Nor was this general harmony (*i. e.* among the Jews) in the least interrupted by the existence of the three prominent sects, which, influenced by their philosophical systems, *differed so much in their interpretation of the Scriptures.*" "The Pharisees approximated very near to the Stoics, the Sadducees to the Epicureans, and the Essenes to the Pythagoreans." Besides, the differences between the followers of *Hillel* and *Shammai*, forming subdivisions of Pharisees, were also tolerated in peace. These parties existed as early as the third century before Christ, and how much earlier other differences may have prevailed is unknown. But nowhere do we read of any *human creed*, proposed for the purpose of forming a separate church organization amongst them.

In the NEW TESTAMENT the revelation from God to man was completed; and although the celebrated Christian father, Origen, informs us that doctrinal differences existed among Christians in the apostolic age, he tells us NOTHING OF ANY HUMAN CREED PROPOSED AT THE TIME.

In the *time of Christ and his Apostles*, the Revelation of God to man was completed, and recorded by the *inspired* Apostles in the New Testament.

* Jahn's Archæology, pl. III., §§ 316, 317.

The system of Christianity was then finished for all after-ages, and for all nations, "till the end of the world." This volume is an infallible rule of faith and practice, and contains an account of the general features of organization of the Church under the inspired Apostles.

With the precepts of this inspired Word, and the outlines of this inspired organization, we hold that the churches of the General Synod of the Evangelical Lutheran Church in the United States are in entire unison, and affirm that they are more successful exemplifications of the proper Church of the New Testament as an inspired, progressive organization for the conversion of sinners and advancement of the kingdom of Christ to its millennial glory, than any other Church of the present age.

When affirming the scriptural character of the General Synod's *doctrinal basis*, we do not mean that it is found in the Word of God in form (*totidem verbis*), but in substance. These sacred oracles were given, not as a text-book of systematic theology, much less, as Hutchinson supposed, of universal science; but as a *popular* revelation, a book of religious instruction for the unlearned masses of the people, as well as for those whose minds had been disciplined by education. Nor is it affirmed that our doctrinal basis is sustained by a command of Scripture, for that sacred volume nowhere enjoins it on the Church to make any uninspired creeds. But it represents itself as complete, and forbids any additions or substitutes with fearful maledictions. "For (says the writer of the Apocalypse) I testify to every man that heareth the words of the prophecy of this book, if any man *shall add unto these things,* God shall *add unto him the plagues* that are written in this book; and if any man shall take away from the words of the book of this prophecy, God shall take away his part out of the book of life, and out of the holy city, and from the things which are written in this book."

But we maintain, that the doctrines expressed in our creed are most manifestly taught in Scripture; that the amount of doctrine required by it for ecclesiastical communion is neither too much nor too little, and is rendered necessary for the preservation of that purity of the church enjoined in God's Word. *What then is the doctrinal basis of the General Synod?* Not the entire mass of the former symbols of Lutheranism in Germany; for these were never all received by many of our European churches. Nor any of all these books but one, namely, the *Augsburg Confession,* which is the only one that was universally received by the Lutheran Church in all parts of Europe.* Nor does the doctrinal basis of the Gen-

* Hutterus Redivivus, p. 116.

eral Synod bind to *every thing* contained in the Augsburg Confession, as has already been stated. The obligation assumed by our ministers at licensure and ordination, as contained in the Constitution for District Synods, published by the General Synod, is in the words: "Do you believe the Scriptures of the Old and New Testament to be the Word of God, and the only infallible rule of faith and practice?"

Do you believe that the *fundamental* doctrines of the Word of God are taught *in a manner substantially correct*, in the doctrinal articles of the Augsburg Confession?

This pledge, in its practical operation, amounts to the reception of the entire Augsburg Confession, except the following topics:—

1. The doctrine of private confession and absolution. 2. The real or literal presence of the body and blood of the Saviour in the Eucharist. 3. Baptismal regeneration. 4. Denial of the divine obligation of the Christian Sabbath. 5. The so-called Ceremonies of the Mass.

This creed is brief, yet comprehensive, and coincides in principle with the so-called Apostles' Creed, and the Nicene Creed, although properly more extended, in order to exclude heretics of later date from the Church. These two creeds sufficed to preserve the doctrinal purity of the Church, as far as creeds can effect this end, during the first five centuries, when the so-called Athanasian Creed gained currency and influence in the Church. From that time till the Reformation, for near 1000 years, these three creeds were generally received by the whole Church, both in its Eastern, or Greek, and in its Western, or Latin or Romish portions,—that is, throughout the entire Christian world, with exception of a few small separate organizations. Some few enactments of successive general councils were of a doctrinal character, but these creeds were regarded as the grand *doctrinal* landmarks of the Christian Church.

As the first two of these creeds are exceedingly interesting, on account of their great antiquity, as well as their universal adoption by the whole Christian Church from the second and fourth centuries, as a fair exposition of what they universally believed the Scriptures to teach, we present them to the reader. These documents also incontestably establish the fact, that the Church, when guided by the inspired apostles, and for several centuries after that period, deemed it lawful to require uniformity only in fundamentals. Several variations occur in the different ancient copies; for example, the phrase in the so-called Apostles' Creed, "*descended into hell,* (or hades, the world of spirits,)" is not found in the earliest copies.

*Apostles' Creed.**

"I believe in God the Father Almighty, the Maker of heaven and earth.

"And in Jesus Christ, his only Son, our Lord, who was conceived by the Holy Ghost, born of the virgin Mary, suffered under Pontius Pilate, was crucified,

* The Apostles' Creed was so called, not because any one in the beginning believed that the apostles had composed it. Had such a belief prevailed, this creed would undoubtedly have been received into *the canon* of the New Testament. For if the apostolic authorship of one apostle invested any book with canonical authority, this creed having, according to a Romish tradition, been the joint work of all the twelve apostles, would have been regarded as possessing the very highest inspiration. For that tradition as related by Ruffinus of the 4th century was, that before the twelve apostles started on their mission to the different nations of the world, they convened at Jerusalem, and composed this creed, each apostle furnishing one sentence of it. But the truth is, the creed was of gradual growth, and was called by the name of the Apostles, because all admitted that the doctrines it contained were those taught by the apostles. The exact age of this creed is unknown. At first it was transmitted by tradition. Ireneus, Tertullian, Origen, and others contain the substance of it, but do not term it a creed. After the formation of the Nicene Creed, on the basis of this ancient traditionary creed or faith of the Church, this also was enlarged, and termed the Faith or Creed of the Apostles; that is, the creed or doctrine which the apostles taught

dead and buried. The third day he rose from the dead, he ascended into heaven, and sitteth on the right hand of God the Father Almighty, whence he shall come to judge the quick and the dead.

"I believe in the Holy Ghost, the holy catholic (that is, universal) Church, the communion of saints, the forgiveness of sins, the resurrection of the body, and life everlasting."

Niceno-Constantinopolitan Creed, A. D. 325 and 381.

"I believe in one God the Father Almighty, Maker of heaven and earth, and of all things visible and invisible.

"And in one Lord Jesus Christ, the only-begotten Son of God, begotten of his Father before all worlds; God of God, Light of Light, true God of the true God, begotten, not made, being of one substance with the Father, by whom all things were made; who for us men, and for our salvation, came down from heaven and was incarnate by the Holy Ghost of the virgin Mary, and was made man, and was crucified also for us under Pontius Pilate. He suffered, and was buried, and the third day he rose again, according to the Scriptures, and ascended into heaven, and sitteth on the right hand of the Father; and he shall come again with glory to judge both the quick and the dead, whose kingdom shall have no end.

"And I believe in the Holy Ghost, the Lord and giver of life, who proceedeth from the Father and the Son, who with the Father and the Son together is worshipped and glorified, who spake by the prophets. And I believe in one catholic (universal) and apostolic Church; I acknowledge one baptism for the remission of sins, and I look for the resurrection of the dead, and the life of the world to come."*

At the time of the glorious Reformation of the 16th century, the truth of these ecumenical or universal symbols, and especially of the first two, was generally conceded. The protest of the reformers was directed against the numberless corruptions of these doctrines, and the superstitious rites and ceremonies which had been added to them. These corrupt additions entirely obscured the moral beauty

* The *Nicene Creed* was adopted by the Council convened by the Emperor Constantine the Great, in A. D. 325, at Nice, a city of Bithynia, in Asia Minor, for the purpose of settling the Arian controversy. The authorship of the creed is by some attributed to Hosius, by others to Hermogenes, and others still to Eusebius of Cæsarea. It was signed by 318 bishops against 17. To this creed several additions were made in A. D. 381, relative to the Holy Spirit, by the Council of Constantinople, convened by the Emperor Theodosius the Great. This council consisted of 150 members, all belonging to the Greek Church. Its object was to oppose the Arians and Macedonians, whose sentiments it condemned.

of the Scripture plan of salvation, by grace through faith in the crucified Redeemer, and substituted a self-righteous system of works, by which unregenerate men were taught to expect admission into that holy heaven, into which no unclean thing can enter.

When the noble-hearted Luther was enlightened by the Spirit of God, to see the errors and corruptions of the Church in which he was born, was educated, and lived till thirty years of age, his good sense led him at once to inquire, By what standard can I correct these errors, and test the whole papal system? By the Fathers of former centuries? No. For, although some of them were good and learned men, they were all fallible. But, thought he, as there is a book, the Bible, professing to be from God, (a book which, providentially, had first greeted his eyes about ten years before, in the twentieth year of his age,) this book must contain the truth unmixed with error, if such truth can be found on earth. He was acquainted with distinguished church fathers of earlier ages, who had taught the Gospel in far greater purity than prevailed in the Church of his day. He was especially attached to the illustrious divine of Hippo, and had joined the Augustinian order called after his name. Thus he might have been tempted to undertake the reformation of the Church on an Augustinian basis, and formed an *Augustinian Church*; but he knew that Christians are commanded to call no *man* Master, well knowing "that one is our Master, even Christ, *i. e.* the Messiah."

Hear his noble protest when his followers began to call the renovated Church after his name, as the Papists had done in derision, led on by the example of Eckius and Pope Adrian.

"I beg," said he, "that men would abstain from using my name, and would call themselves, *not Lutherans* but *Christians*. What is Luther? My doctrine is not mine. Neither was I crucified for any one. Paul would not suffer Christians to be called either after him or Peter, but after Christ (1 *Cor.* iii. 4, 5). Why should it happen to me, poor corruptible food of worms, that the disciples of Christ should be called after my abominable name? Be it not so, beloved friends, but let us *extirpate party names*, and be called Christians; for it is the doctrine of Christ that we teach." *

Luther therefore asserted the long suppressed right of private judgment, that *lever* of the Reformation, and adopted the Bible as the only infallible guide and test, not only for the removal of the

* Luther's Works, vol. xviii. p. 293, 6th Leipsic edition. See also the author's Fraternal Appeal to the American Churches, with a Plan for Catholic Union on Protestant Principles. p. 69. New York: 1839. 2d edit.

errors and superstitions of Romanism, but also to direct him in the reorganization of the Church, and in all his actions in life. By this standard he continued to investigate the whole field of Romish doctrine and practice. Although he had *taken an oath*, at the time the theological doctorate was conferred on him, to teach no other doctrines than those prescribed by the Romish Church, yet when he saw that Rome had corrupted the doctrines of the gospel, he unhesitatingly denounced her corruptions.

He saw intuitively, that an oath taken to perform an act subsequently seen to be sinful, cannot be binding.* This noble work of Reformation he continued to prosecute until the close of his life, *binding himself to no creed except the Bible.* Hence, though in a certain sense, Luther may be regarded as the author of the Reformation, and the founder of the Church that bears his name, yet, with the

* This principle has been acted on both by Romanists and Protestants of more recent date. Joachim II., Elector of Brandenburg, bound himself to his father, by the honor and the oath of a prince, on behalf of himself and his heirs, to remain true to the Romish Church; and yet he was swept along with the victorious current of the Lutheran Reformation. On the other hand, John Sigismund pledged himself to his father with an oath, never to forsake Luther's doctrines, and yet, in 1614, abandoned the doctrine of the real presence, and could find peace only in the view of the Reformed Church on this subject.

great Apostle, he could justly have said, "I neither received it of man, neither was I taught it, but by the revelation of Jesus Christ." And it should be remembered, that although different confessions (the former symbolical books) were published by the Reformers, containing a statement of their belief, and Luther himself had signed one of them, not one, except the Form of Concord, was written *for the purpose* of being made binding on the ministers of the Church: nor were they generally made thus binding until after both Luther and Melanchthon had gone to their eternal rest. Then (in 1580) the Form of Concord was published, and together with the other Confessions was made symbolical; that is, made binding on the ministers of the Church, not by the Church herself, but by the civil authorities. This was thirty-four years after Luther's death, and twenty years after that of Melanchthon. *Let it then be remembered that Luther, though he believed the contents of the symbolic books to be true, never bound himself to them, nor was the Church as a body so bound by them, till a quarter of a century after his death.* In short, neither the names of fallible men, nor trans-fundamental creeds ought ever to be imposed as binding on the Church of Christ.

Had Luther's advice been accepted and his name not been employed to designate the Church of Christ, which he was instrumental in purifying, the common argument would have fallen to the ground, which many of our symbolic friends are wont to regard as unanswerable: namely, that those alone can consistently belong to the Lutheran Church, who believe all the doctrines which Luther believed. How differently would this argument strike all honest readers, if stated thus: Those alone can consistently belong to the Evangelical Church, that is, the Church founded on the *gospel,* who believe, not all that the gospel teaches, but all that Luther taught. Evidently here a fallible man is virtually made the *principium cognoscendi,* the source of knowledge, of a Christian Church, instead of the inspired gospel of God! This use of personal names is justly rebuked by the Apostle Paul, for it has been the prolific source of much evil. The Scriptures alone are designed to be our infallible rule of faith and practice; and as long as the Church lasts on earth, it is her duty to study that Word, and faithfully to act out her convictions of its teachings. The Bible represents itself as the only infallible rule (*Revel.* xxii. 18, 19); but our symbolic friends point us to the Bible only as understood and explained by Luther, or the symbolical books which form a mass of human prescription, equal in size to the whole Old Testament, composed by good and learned but fallible men, at a time when sacred philology and exegesis were in their infancy!!

Nor should Christians ever consent to bind themselves unchangeably to such *extended trans-fundamental* creeds. The Bible alone is infallible truth, unmixed with error, that is, *objective* truth. All human creeds are only *subjective,* are truth as apprehended by the minds of men. Since men are depraved and fallible, it might in advance be expected that their subjective creeds would be tarnished by some error. But that they positively and certainly are mingled with it, is demonstrated by the fact, that on many, especially on non-fundamental doctrines, the leading creeds extant in the world, present *opposite instructions;* and of two different and opposite teachings or doctrines, one only can be true. History moreover teaches, that the creeds of the different *Evangelical* Churches *agree* as to *fundamental,* and differ chiefly in non-fundamental doctrines. Hence only fundamental doctrines should be admitted into public creeds to be made binding; and if any denomination adds other doctrines of non-fundamental character, viz., her own denominational peculiarities, these should confessedly be regarded in a different light, as constantly open to improvement, whenever the increasing light of biblical science may demand. Do you say this is a dangerous position? It is advocated even by the Form of Concord itself: "But (say its authors) the other symbols and writings cited, are not judges as the

Scriptures are, but are only evidence or declaration of the faith, to show how at all times the Scriptures, in reference to articles disputed in the Church of God, were understood and explained by *the persons then living*, and how the opposite doctrines were rejected and condemned." * The Reformers acknowledged the duty of "searching the Scriptures," and vindicated to themselves the right to "prove all things and hold fast that which is good." Nor did they dream of denying the same right to after-ages. But the unhappy union of Church and State incorporated these Confessions into the ecclesiastical laws of the land, punishing any denial of them with civil penalties, and thus closing the door to all subsequent amendment of them.

In our own happy country, Church and State are divorced, and here the Church has power to exercise her natural rights, and we add, is bound to do so.

Our General Synod has accordingly returned to the high and truly noble principles of Luther. Believing the Bible alone to be the infallible rule of

* Die andern Symbola aber, und angezogene Schriften, sind nicht Richter wie die heilige Schrift, sondern allein Zeugnis und Erklärung des Glaubens, wie jederzeit die heilige Schrift in streitigen Artikeln in der Kirche Gottes von den damals lebenden verstanden und ausgelegt, und derselbige widerwertige Lehre verworfen und verdammet worden."—Müller's Symbolische Bücher, p. 518.

faith and practice, she yet approves of the great mass of the doctrines taught in the symbolical books, because she regards them as constituting the divine plan of salvation taught in God's Word; and she dissents from several minor doctrines, for which she can find no Scriptural authority; as Luther himself did in regard to some of the concessions made by Melanchthon to the Papists, in the Augsburg Confession.* Desiring to have some creed, as well

* On the 22d of June, the day after the public presentation of the Confession, he (Melanchthon) again addresses Luther: "We live here in *the most lamentable anxiety and incessant tears.*" During the entire six weeks that Melanchthon was at Augsburg before the arrival of the Emperor, his mind was in this agitated and alarmed condition. According to his own account, he continued daily to make changes in the Confession to appease the Romanists, *after* it had been submitted to Luther. No wonder, therefore, that Luther, responding to Melanchthon's inquiry, "*what more they could yield to the Romanists,*" makes this rather dissatisfied reply: "*Your Apology* (the Augsburg Confession, as altered by Melanchthon after Luther had sanctioned it on the 15th of May, and it had been presented to the Diet on the 25th of June) *I have received, and I wonder what you mean, when you desire to know what and how much may be yielded to the Papists. As far as I am concerned,* TOO MUCH HAS ALREADY BEEN YIELDED TO THEM IN THE APOLOGY (THE CONFESSION): [für meine Person ist ihnen *allzuviel* nachgegeben in der Apologia (Confession).] Luther's Werke, B. xx., p. 185. Leipsic Edit. "*I daily altered and recast the greater part of it,* (says Melanchthon himself,) *and would have altered still more, if our*

as to bear witness to the truth as it is in Jesus, as also to preserve the purity of the Church, she professes to regard the *Augsburg Confession* as a cor-

counsellors would have allowed it." But Melanchthon and his associates were willing to make still more important concessions, *after* the Confession had been delivered; so that Luther, in a letter dated Sept. 20th, to *Justus Jonas*, one of the principal Protestant theologians at the Diet, gives vent to his feelings in the following remarkable language: "*I almost burst with anger and displeasure,* (*Ich börste schier für Zorn und Widerwillen,*) *and I beg you only to cut short the matter, cease to negotiate with them* (the Papists) *any longer, and come home. They have the Confession. They have the gospel. If they are willing to yield to it, then it is well. If they are unwilling to yield to it, they may go.* IF WAR COMES OUT OF IT, LET IT COME. *We have entreated and done enough. The Lord has prepared them as victims for the slaughter, that he may reward them according to their works. But us, his people, he will deliver, even if we were sitting in the fiery furnace at Babylon.*" Luther's Works, vol. xx. p. 196.

Well has the historian Arnold said, "Melanchthon had prepared the Confession amid great fear and trembling, and in many things accommodated himself to the Papists." Kirche und Ketzer Geschichte, vol. I. p. 809, 2d ed. of 1740.

The distinguished historian, Professor Schrœck, testifies to the same fact. "Every one knows (says he) that this confession of faith, known as the Augsburg Confession, is the principal symbolical book of the Evangelical (Lutheran) Church. But few of those who have heard it mentioned, or have cursorily glanced at it, are aware how *designedly it tendered a reconciliation* to the Romish Church, and facili-

rect exhibition of the *fundamental* doctrines of the Word of God. And the friends of the General Synod finding themselves in unison with the doctrines and usages of the Lutheran Church *in all essential points*, and much attached to them, continue to retain the name of Luther, and labor in the Church of their fathers. When the patriarchs of American Lutheranism first established churches in this country, about a century and a quarter ago, they at first continued the practice then prevailing in Halle, whence most of them came, of requiring from candidates for the ministry a pledge to all the Symbolical books then in force in Saxony. But they soon began to discriminate between the Augsburg Confession and the other books. About the close of the last century they ceased to require any such pledge, even to the Augsburg Confession.

tated such a result." Vol. I. p. 447, of his Christliche Kirchengeschichte seit der Reformation.

Here then we have the most unequivocal testimony of *Luther himself*, as well as of concurrent historians, that the Augsburg Confession still retains concessions to popery, to which he was opposed. Probably some of the several points in that Confession, to which American Lutherans still object, may have been among these concessions, especially the language applied to the Mass, so much milder than that applied to it by Luther himself in his Smalcald Articles.

See also Schmucker's Lutheran Symbols, or Vindication of American Lutheranism, p. 53, 2d edit.

When we were admitted to the ministry by the Pennsylvania Synod, in the spring of 1820, not a word was said to us of any symbol. Nor was the Confession officially avowed, by the requisition of assent to it, even by the Pennsylvania Synod or any other, from that time until the third meeting of the General Synod in 1825, when it was the privilege of the present writer to present the so-called *Statutes* of the Theological Seminary, then adopted by that body, containing the following words: "In this seminary shall be taught, in the German and English languages, the *fundamental* doctrines of the Sacred Scriptures, as contained in the Augsburg Confession." And in the Constitution of the Seminary the same obligation is repeated, in the same language, and also in terms somewhat varied, though synonymous, in Article I. of the Constitution, § 2: "The design of this Institution shall be, to train up ministers who sincerely believe and cordially approve of the doctrines of the Holy Scriptures, as they are *fundamentally taught* in the Augsburg Confession;" and likewise in the Constitution for District Synods, published by the General Synod, at Licensure and Ordination.

By this qualified, though essential avowal of the Augsburg Confession, the General Synod professes her historical connection with the Church of the Reformation, as well as of the Nicene and earlier ages, and has a test by which she can exclude fundamental error from the Church; whilst she reserves to her members the liberty of the primitive and Ante-Nicene period, of differing on non-fundamental topics, without crimination, or disturbance of ecclesiastical relations. This liberal basis seems also accordant with the instructions of the great apostle of the Gentiles, "to receive," and not reject, "a brother that is weak in *the* faith;" that is, erroneous, in our judgment, in some minor points, which do not prevent him from being a "*brother;*" but not for the purpose of disputation on doubtful topics. It also approximates the advice of the illustrious champion of the truth, the great Athanasius, and other Nicene Fathers of the fourth century, who regarded the creed issued by that celebrated council as sufficient for all ages to come. "*That faith* (says Athanasius) *which those fathers there confessed, was sufficient for the refutation of all impiety, and the establishment of all faith in Christ and true religion.*"* The emperor Zeno also wrote an epistle, *Enotikon,*† or, The Epistle of *Reconciliation,* in which Christians are invited to unite in receiving the Nicene Creed; and it is added, that

* Epist. ad Epict.—"Η γᾶρ ἐν ἀυτῇ παρὰ τῶν πατέρων κατα τὰς θείας γραφὰς ὁμολογηθεῖσα πίςτις, ἀυτάκρης ἐςτὶ προς ἀνατροπην μεν πάσης ασεβείας, σύδασιν δε τῆς ἐυσεβειας ἐν Χριδῳ πι-τεως.

† Evag. lib. iii c. 14.

"*the Church should never receive any other creed.*" This basis is also adapted to the millennial era of the Church, receiving into her fold all who give evidence of Christian character, and agree so far with us in doctrine, mode of worship, and government, as to be able to co-operate harmoniously with us. So, also, *Acts* ii. 17, Peter said concerning the Gentiles who had received the Holy Ghost, "Forasmuch as God gave them the like gift as he did unto us, who believed on the Lord Jesus Christ, what was I that I could withstand God?" Had the civil rulers of Germany, when they arrogated to themselves the power of prescribing a creed, and of compelling all ministers to bind themselves to its support, adopted the doctrinal articles, or even the whole, of the Augsburg Confession,—omitting three or four disputed points of minor moment,—instead of the entire mass of symbolic books, forming a volume of about 600 pages, equal to the entire Old Testament, there would have been far less controversy in our Churches in Europe, and the Lutheran Church this day would number millions of members more than she now does. In confirmation of this opinion, it may be stated that the Church of England, which adopted a creed (the Thirty-nine Articles) of the length recommended, about eighteen years before the Book of Concord was adopted, though she has had, perhaps, as great a diversity of doctrinal views in her ministry as has been found in the Lutheran Church, has not been distracted by one-fourth part as many or as bitter doctrinal controversies. And of the Methodist Church in America, it is still more worthy of remark, that she struck out from the *Thirty-Nine Articles* several of the remaining disputed topics; and though she counts 1,000,000 of members, she has been disturbed by no doctrinal controversies at all, and has increased more rapidly than any other Church in our land.*

The principal doctrines actually received by the ministry of the General Synod, and required by their doctrinal basis, are the following:—

I. The Unity of the Godhead in a Trinity of Persons.

II. The proper and eternal Divinity of the Son of God, our Saviour, Jesus Christ.

III. The Total Depravity of our race in consequence of the Fall.

IV. The Incarnation of the Son of God, and his Vicarious Atonement for the sins of the world.

V. Justification, not by works, but by grace alone, through faith.

VI. Regeneration by the Holy Ghost, through the truth, and good works, as the fruit and evidence of our faith.

* The Thirty-nine Articles were adopted in 1562, and the Book of Concord in 1580.

VII. The divine institution and perpetuity of the Gospel Ministry, of the Lord's Day or Christian Sabbath, and of the sacraments of Baptism and the Holy Supper.

VIII. The Immortality of the soul, and Judgment of the world by our Lord Jesus Christ.

IX. The eternal blessedness of the righteous.

X. The everlasting punishment of the wicked.

In addition to these fundamental truths, the doctrines of Pedo-Baptism, and universality of the Atonement, taught in the Confession, are received by all the Churches of the General Synod.

Of the doctrine of the redemption of the world through the eternal Son of God, our Churches entertain the most exalted view. They hold that Christ tasted death literally for *every one*, (*Heb.* ii. 9, παντι,) and that this redemption is complete; so that, on account of it, all children who die in infancy, before the years of moral agency, will be saved, as also that all who reach the age of responsibility are in a salvable state, in which, though depraved by nature, and liable to condemnation on account of personal sins, they may be saved by the performance of certain conditions made possible by Divine grace to all who hear the Gospel. These conditions are suited to the capacities of each individual; and though different from the conditions of our first parents in Eden, they are equally just and impartial to all. Our pardon and justification are, moreover, entirely of grace, and in no degree the result of our works or sufferings.

"Our sin can ne'er be crucified
By cross or suffering of our own:
The cross whereon Immanuel died
Alone can win the victor's crown.

"We own but *one Gethsemane*,
And there the debt of woe was paid;
We know but *one true Calvary*,
And there was sin's atonement made."

As our justification is not by works, it need not be delayed till after some period of holy living, but it follows *instantly* on the performance of the *first* act of living faith. "Now is the accepted time; now is the day of salvation."

And when we have thus been justified by faith, we have peace with God,—have the testimony of the Spirit, bearing witness with our spirits, that we are children of God.—*Rom.* viii. 14.

These fundamental doctrines form the moral bond which unites into one totality all the disciples of our Divine Master of every land. They constitute that galaxy of divine truth by which the Holy Spirit has illuminated a large part of the world, has banished ignorance, superstition, and idolatry from the nations now Christian, has lifted the veil and revealed to them in some measure the structure of the invisible world, and by which he has illuminated, convicted, converted, sanctified and saved millions of our fellow-men. It is this truth, also, which will extend its radiations from the throne of God to the remotest dark places of the earth, gloriously illustrating the moral government of Jehovah over heaven, earth and hell. Under the free development secured by the principles of the General Synod, the American Lutheran Church is *eclectic* in its features, and occupies a kind of middle or common ground between the other evangelical denominations. She may be emphatically styled the *Church of the Reformation.* She holds the grand doctrines of Christianity, with fewer appended peculiarities than most other denominations. With the Calvinist, she holds the graciousness of salvation; with the Congregationalist, she believes that Christ tasted death for every man; with the Methodist, she approves of regularly recurring protracted meetings; with the Episcopalians, she occasionally employs a liturgy, with forms of prayer; with the German Reformed, she agrees in the instruction and confirmation of catechumens; and with all she unites in ascribing all the glory of our privileges on earth and hopes in heaven to the Lamb of God that taketh away the sins of the world. Long may these blessed doctrines be taught in our Churches throughout our land and throughout the world, until all who love the Lord indeed unite in proclaiming the truth: one is our Master, Christ, and we are all brethren. How noble, therefore, is the doctrinal basis of our General Synod!

CHAPTER IX.

The General Synod's Views of Government and Discipline are Scriptural.

THE earliest organization of the visible Church of God in the Old Testament was elementary and progressive. Some few features of visibility may be observed in the period immediately succeeding the Fall, in the observance of the Sabbath, and offering of sacrifices as early as the time of Cain and Abel, when the pater-familias seems to have been the only religious teacher. In *Genesis* iv. 26, also, we have an intimation of the early existence of the Church, or worshipping people of God. "And to Seth, to him also there was born a son; and he called his name Enos: *then began men to call upon the name of the Lord.*" The Patriarchal organization seems to confer some visibility on the earliest Church of God; and this probably continued, during the antediluvian period, amongst all who sustained any worship at all. The late Dr. J. M. Mason, of New

York, one of the ablest divines our country has produced, did indeed maintain that God had no *visible* Church on earth until the appointment of the Aaronic priesthood, and others, as Dr. Randal, of the Episcopal Church, until the time of Abraham; but this dispute resolves itself into mere logomacy. That the true worshippers of God, in all ages, were the invisible or spiritual Church of God, will not be disputed. And as the New Testament tells us of the church in the family of Aquila and Priscilla,* and in the house of Nymphas,† and also in the house of Philemon,‡ we may with perfect propriety also designate similar worshipping families in the earlier period of the Old Testament Churches of God. In later periods, the worship assumed a more collective and diversified form, as well as a more definite local habitation, in the tabernacle, the temple, and the synagogue, in which reading of the Law, the Prophets, and the Psalms became the prominent part. The *Mosaic* economy was characterized by the priesthood, the reading of the Old Testament, and the ceremonial worship,—the first and last being typical and superseded in the New Testament. Under the Christian dispensation the organization of the visible church was completed, but is still distinguished by its simplicity and unostentatiousness.

In the primitive Church of Christ, the system of

* 1 Cor. xvi. 19. † 2 Col. iv. 15. ‡ Philemon 2.

the *synagogue* was the model for its permanent organization. "It is well known," says Dr. Winer, "that the earlier meetings of Christians for worship on the Lord's Day were organized after the model of the synagogue worship; and in *James* ii. 2 such an assemblage is termed a synagogue (συναγωγή), although it remains still undecided, whether that name is employed as a permanent name derived from the Jews, or is to be understood in its appellative sense," to signify an assemblage. — *Winer's Biblical Lexicon*, vol. ii. *p.* 551.

The Apostles were evidently *temporary* officers, appointed by the Saviour for a special purpose, namely, to substantiate the divinity of his religion by miracles, and "to testify to the resurrection of Christ."* Accordingly, they were to be selected, said the apostle Peter, from among those "which have companied with us all the time that the Lord Jesus went in and out among us, beginning from the baptism of John, unto that same day that he was taken up from us." *

The permanent officers of the Church were, first, Elders, (sometimes also termed bishops, pastors, &c.,) all of which terms, during the first century, designated the same officer; and, secondly, *Deacons*, (lay officers,) whose duties, as the evangelist Luke informs us, were to serve at tables, to make the dis-

* Acts. i. 22. † Acts i. 21

tribution of provisions and money contributed for the poor widows of the Church. Thus they relieved the apostles from this service, that they might devote their time wholly "to the preaching of the word and to prayers." Of course, an order of men appointed expressly to perform secular and not clerical duties, must be a secular or lay order; although there can be no reason why some of them may not subsequently have advanced to the ministerial office, as in the case of Philip. *Acts* vii. 5, 6. In some Churches, also, there were *Deaconesses,* whose duty it was to perform the same services to poor and sick females in the Church for which deacons were originally appointed among the males. These deaconesses were selected from the pious widows of the Church who were over sixty years of age. "I commend unto you," says Paul, "Phœbe, our sister, who is a servant (οὖσαν διάκονον is *a deaconess*) of the Church at Cenchrea." And again: "Let *not* a widow be taken into the number, *under three-score years old,* having been the wife of one man, well reported of for good works." *Rom.* xvi. 1; 1 *Tim.* v. 9. These deaconesses remained at home, and labored in the congregation by which they were selected. Of a number of deaconesses, young and old, collected together in some one institution, we have no example in the Word of God. The celebrated Roman writer Pliny the younger, mentions deaconesses among the Christians of his day, A. D. 107, in his Epistle to the Emperor Trajan. See Dr. Lardner's Works, vol. vii. pp. 293, 313, 341.

In the apostolic age, the different congregations were all independent of each other, each having final control of its own affairs. The calling of a *council* for mutual consultation, (an account of which we find in the 15th chapter of the *Acts*,) gives sanction to the general principle, and justifies similar convocations as often as experience proves them to be necessary and useful.

But in the *apostolic age* there were no synods, in the modern sense of the term; that is, no meetings consisting of all the ministers, or even representatives of them, and lay delegates of the Churches, within a given district, and meeting statedly; as all the Churches were, at that time, *independent.*

In the *second* century, the term bishop (ἐπίσκοπος), which had before been used as synonymous with elder (πρεσβυτερος), to signify the ordinary ministers of the Church, began to acquire a special usage and meaning, to designate the ministers who presided at their occasional meetings as *primus inter pares,* and especially those resident in larger towns or cities, who acquired first a moral influence, and afterwards an official oversight over the ministers in the surrounding country (*chorepiscopoi.*) This was the origin of *diocesan episcopacy.** In large cities, also, where one church was not sufficient, several associated churches were established, and thus a diocese was formed around the bishop.

Synods were not introduced into the Church until the latter half of the second century, when we meet them in the Eastern or Greek Church, which had been familiar with the Amphictyonic councils in their civil government. Sometimes the bishops of a particular province of the empire convened and held a *Provincial Synod;* at others, the bishops of the whole country were invited to assemble in the national metropolis; on which occasions the metropolitan, or chief minister of the metropolis, presided, and the synod was termed a *Metropolitan Synod, or Council.* Properly speaking, these meetings were councils, rather than regularly returning synods, and all the meetings were generally constituted of *bishops and clergy alone*, the laity having been ordinarily excluded. In the *fifth century*, the dignity of *Patriarch* was given to the bishops of five principal cities,—Rome, Constantinople, Jerusalem, &c.,—each incumbent having supervision over the bishops within his province, and being alone competent to ordain the bishops in his district. The

* For particulars and proof, see the author's Popular Theology, 9th ed., pp. 221–226.

Pope of Rome, however, established his power over them all, in the next century.

The climax of imparity was attained, and the rights of the laity finally obliterated, when, in the commencement of the *seventh century* (606), *the papacy* was established, and the subjugation of the Church to the papal hierarchy completed. This condition, so different from that of the primitive organization of the disciples of the meek and lowly Saviour, continued, with various fluctuations, until the glorious Reformation of the sixteenth century.

The *Protestant Churches* at that time all rejected the dominion of the Pope, but they failed to attain the primitive independence of all State control, which characterized the Churches prior to the union of Church and State, under Constantine the Great, in the fourth century. Indeed, it was the power of their civil rulers which saved them from utter ruin by the minions of the Pope of Rome; and that same power was necessary for their continued protection. But the idea of protecting them as citizens, and then permitting them to regulate their own ecclesiastical affairs, was not yet understood, either by the princes or the people. The civil government, therefore, by common consent, undertook to regulate all the external affairs of the Church, such as the erection of church edifices, selection and appointment of ministers, as well as paying their salary, &c. The ecclesiastical affairs in Protestant Europe are usually confided to a mixed commission, called *Consistorium*, consisting of several civilians representing the State, and several theologians representing the Church; but all are selected by the king, and salaried by him. This form of governing the affairs of the Church has continued in all the Protestant kingdoms of Europe till this day.

Exercising the liberty allowed to all Churches in things not defined in the Scriptures, the Churches of the General Synod of the Evangelical Lutheran Church have adopted three forms of associated government, namely: the Council (or vestry, or session of every local Church), District Synods (consisting of all the ministers within certain geographical limits, and a lay delegate from each pastoral district, meeting once a year and exercising supervision and control over the pastors and churches within their bounds), and, lastly, the General Synod. The latter body was formed in 1820, at Hagerstown, Maryland, and meets at least once in three years. In general, it has met biennially, and consists of delegates from all the different District Synods connected with it, according to a fixed ratio of representation. Its powers are chiefly *advisory*, and its principal duties are to inspect the ministers of the District Synods, in order to exert a favorable influence on the Church at large.

It is also recommended that each District Synod be divided into several *Special Conferences*, for the purpose of spending several days in close practical preaching, to awaken and convert sinners, and edify believers.

The views of the General Synod of our American Lutheran Zion on this subject are officially set forth in the Formula of Government and Discipline, published by said body, and annexed to our hymn-book.

A prominent feature of this system is *Ministerial Parity*. The leading reformers of the 16th century regarded the form of church government as of minor moment, and not defined as to its details in Scripture. Hence, whilst all our divines, as *Dr. Mosheim* informs us,* admitted ministerial parity to have been the primitive system, their civil governments adopted different forms for themselves, on the ground of expediency. In Germany, where the Reformation was commenced, and principally conducted by the theologians, the existing episcopacy was abolished, and virtual parity maintained. But in Denmark, Norway, and Sweden, where the kings were movers and chief conductors of the work, episcopacy was retained, as more consonant with existing regal forms of government.

* Ecclesiastical History, Murdock's Translation, vol. iii. p. 130.

In Europe our Church has, until recently, had no regular Synods, and even those of late years allowed by the civil governments of Germany, are not equal representations of the churches generally and are controlled by the civil governments. Our American fathers, however, introduced the regular synodical system in 1748, soon after the organization of our Church in this country, thus adopting a *Republican* form of government, as more congenial to our civil institutions,* as had been done by the Presbyterian Churches around them.

As to *Church Discipline,* properly so called, the

* Several years before the American Revolution, there was a Baptist church near the house of Mr. Thos. Jefferson, in Virginia, which was governed on congregational principles, whose monthly meetings he occasionally attended. He expressed himself much interested in its government, and said he considered it the only pure form of democracy then existing in the world, and best adapted for the government of the American colonies. See Encyc. Rel. Knowledge, art. Congregationalism; Syke's Lecture on the Baptist Church. This idea of democratic self-government has become incorporated with our entire system of civil government, and also pervades the greater part of the ecclesiastical organizations of our land, such as the Lutheran, the Presbyterian, the Reformed, the Baptist, and the Congregational. On the other hand, the Methodist Episcopal, and the Protestant Episcopal Churches retain some features of aristocracy, whilst the Romish Church is everywhere governed on principles essentially monarchical.

illustrious reformers of the 16th century were so hampered by the influence of their civil rulers, many of whom, though co-workers in the reformation from popery, were not consistent Christians in their life, that they did not introduce or prepare anything like a complete scriptural discipline. Different cities and principalities adopted different directories for worship, including a few disciplinarian regulations, but nothing that can be regarded as a scriptural and complete system of discipline. And when the Bohemian brethren, in 1522, and again in 1523, sent deputations to Luther, to encourage him in his great work, as well as to induce him to prepare and introduce a better system of discipline into his churches, he gave them this memorable reply: "We cannot yet attain unto it, that we should require such a practice of our doctrines, and of holiness of life, as we hear that you do. Amongst us things are yet too crude, and proceed slowly; but pray for us."*

Unfortunately nothing effectual, or near the scriptural standard, has been generally introduced into any of the established churches on the continent of Europe to this day.† In this country the

* Loretz, Ratio Disciplinæ Unitatis Fratrum, p. 62.

† Thus in the church at Basel, in Switzerland, the writer was informed, in 1846, by the celebrated Dr. De Wette, that a certain senator was a *notorious* libertine, and had seduced

founders of our Church introduced a far better set of rules in some of their churches, and in 1823, the General Synod adopted the Formula for the government and discipline of individual churches, prepared by the Synod of Maryland and Virginia, in 1822.

In 1827, the General Synod appointed a Committee to prepare a Constitution for the Government and Discipline of the District Synods. These two, together with the Constitution of the General Synod, constitute *a complete system of government and discipline* of the Scripture standard. The General Synod is in most matters an advisory council, although in regard to several specified cases, it may act as a court of appeals, and exercise more active powers. It is probable that, in accordance with the original design of the Plan of 1819, stronger powers will be conferred on it by the revised constitution, to be reported at the next meeting of the body, in order to secure greater uniformity of the books and forms of public worship. Under this system of discipline the churches have improved in spirituality, and increased in numbers, more rapidly than at any previous time. This improvement also in every congregation is proportioned to the degree of fidelity with which the Formula has been carried out by

several of his own domestics; yet he regularly took h's place in church, and approached the table of the Lord unadmonished the pastor and church council. The moral influence of the churches upon the surrounding world has been far more salutary, and professing Christians appear as "lights of the world" and as "salt of the earth." In regard to government and discipline, therefore, our General Synod may also be confidently pronounced *accordant with God's Word,* as it adopts all its specific precepts, and conforms to its spirit in all things else.

CHAPTER X.

The Mode of Worship of the General Synod is accordant with Scripture.

N the primitive and patriarchal age of the Old Testament, the worship of God was extremely simple, consisting of prayer, sacrifices, religious instructions, and the observance of the Sabbath. The paterfamilias, as we have above stated, was the priest of the household, and the place of worship was the private dwelling of each, as also adjoining groves and hills.

In the *New Testament* the appointed parts of the service were the reading of the Scriptures, preaching, or the expounding of the portion read, singing of psalms, hymns and spiritual songs, and prayer. All these exercises, except the reading of the Word of God, were extemporaneous,—that is, original, peculiar, and new for each occasion, though they may have been, and *doubtless often were, premeditated*. The individual personality of the speaker seems, in the economy of grace, designed to add increased power to the truth. The sentiments of the prayers and discourses, uttered from his heart, afford stronger proof of the speaker's self-conviction and sincerity than if he merely reads what others have written. Moreover, constant variety in every exercise seems to interest more deeply the feelings of the hearers. If the uniform repetition of the same prayer is favorable to devotion and edification, would it not be natural to expect that the constant repetition of one or several well prepared sermons, read by all preachers every Sabbath, through a lifetime, would also be productive of greater results, than when each preacher presents his own sermons, and rarely repeats even these, until after the lapse of years?

The preaching was ordinarily performed by the apostles and elders, or bishops, as it now is in the churches of the General Synod by the stated ministry. Yet on some occasions, we read of others, who were moved by the Spirit to utter words of exhortation; and so in the prayer-meeting and private conference for edification, we suppose, that by virtue of the universal priesthood of believers, (1 *Pet.* ii. 9, *Rev.* i. 6; v. 10,) pious and exemplary Christian laymen, if moved by a sense of duty, may publicly read the Scriptures, and utter words of admonition, or read an approved sermon, when there is no minister present to preach.

The prayers offered were also extemporaneous, or, as Justin Martyr (A. D. 138) says, "the presiding officer or minister prays *according to his ability*,"* (ὄση δύναμις ἀυτῷ;) or, as Tertullian says, (*ex proprio ingenio*,) "from his own mind." The more detailed statement of Justin Martyr is the following: "On the day called Sunday, we all assemble together, both those who reside in the country and they who dwell in the city, and the Commentaries of the apostles, and the writings of the prophets, are read as long as time permits. When the reader has ended, the president, or minister, in an address, makes an application, and enforces an imitation of the excellent things which have been read. *Then we all stand up together, and offer up our prayers.* After our prayers, as I have said, bread and wine and water are brought, and the president, in like manner, offers prayers and thanksgivings *according to his ability*, (ὄση δύναμις ἀυτῷ,) and the people respond, saying Amen," (that is, so be it). Here we find no indication whatever of the use of written forms of prayer, and all translations of these words, designed to teach the contrary, are forced and unsustained by the *usus loguendi* of the authors. *Nor do the Scriptures contain a single prayer or other form which was written before it was offered* The few sentences

* Apology, I. c. 13, pp. 50, 51. *Apud* Coleman, Primitive Church, p. 341.

prescribed for the offering of the first-fruits, (*Deut.* xxvi. 5–15,) and at the payment of tithes (xxvi. 13–15,) were not forms for ordinary public worship. When Solomon offered the dedicatory prayer in the Temple, "he spread forth his hands towards heaven," and could not have held a book or manuscript prayer in them, and it was evidently taken down afterwards, or, if written, was delivered from memory. Even the Lord's Prayer, which was expressly given by the Saviour to "instruct the disciples how to pray," seems rather to have been intended to teach us the proper *subjects*, the condensed and simple *mode* and the filial *spirit*, than to serve as a complete form of Christian prayer. For it contains no reference to the great work of redemption, or salvation by grace, nor are the petitions offered in the name of the Redeemer. Moreover, there are no traces in the New Testament of its having ever been actually employed by any of the Apostles, or first Christians. Nor does history teach us that it was used in public worship after the apostolic age, till the close of the second century. All this clearly proves the opinion of Augustine to be true, that it was not given as a *set form* of prayer, nor so employed by the primitive Christians;* whilst our Church very properly

* The celebrated Augustine maintains this view: "Non enim *verba*, sed res ipsas eos verbis docuit, quibus et se ipsi, a quo et quid esset orandum cum in penetralibus, ut dictum, mentis orarent." De Magistro, c. 2, vol. I. p. 402.

urges its occasional use in connection with extemporary prayer.

If, as has been asserted, the Jews used written forms of prayers at ordinary public worship, the example of such a corrupt Church, so emphatically condemned by the Saviour,* could not be binding on us without a divine command.

Authentic history informs us, according to the most recent and learned investigations, that written prayers or liturgies were introduced generally in the fourth and fifth centuries, to aid incompetent ministers, who could not well conduct the public services without them. *Siegel,* a recent German archæologist of high reputation,† says: "After the distinguished Christian teachers had passed from the stage, and had been succeeded by others of inferior education,—when barbarism and ignorance were making continued inroads on the Roman Empire, and the mysterious portions ‡ of worship in a measure disappeared from Christianity,—then the clergy who felt unequal to the task of animating the religious assemblies by their own powers of mind, found themselves compelled to have recourse to written

Matt. vi. 7; viii. 23, 14.

† Siegel's Handbuch der Christlich-kirchlichen Alterthümer, vol. iii. p. 205.

‡ Certain secret rites borrowed from the heathen mysteries.

directories, which were soon composed and furnished by obliging individuals."—"These were fictitiously attributed to distinguished men, and even to Apostles, in order to confer on them greater importance. Most probably the *close of the fifth century* is the period at which it became customary to write down these formularies."

"The industry of Bigham, who labors to prove from individual passages that such standing written formularies had existed as early as the second century, is unavailing. For those passages accurately examined, either do not establish the point in question, or they refer only to individual, rare cases, which cannot prove the existence of a general custom." Thus far the testimony of *Siegel.* Since, therefore, liturgies are without Scripture authority, and all parts of Christian worship in the apostolic and immediately succeeding ages were extemporaneous, or though premeditated and possibly written in a few cases, yet not read from a manuscript or copy, we should be careful not essentially to change that mode of worship. And yet a brief liturgy, the use of which is left optional, may be useful in several respects. First, its private perusal and study by young ministers may make them acquainted with the order of exercises, which should constitute the public worship, as well as all other ministerial acts, and familiarize them with the trains of thought, of which each should consist. And, secondly, a brief introductory service read, always combined with *extemporary* prayer, produces a desirable uniformity in public worship, and leaves the general extemporary and scriptural character of the services materially unchanged. Judicious *rubrics* also tend greatly to produce uniformity and instruct both ministers and the laity how to perform their duties. Those reported in the Liturgy provisionally adopted by the General Synod in 1866, were prepared with great care. Now precisely this is the nature, and this the use of the General Synod's Liturgy, being substantially that of the patriarchs of our American forefathers, somewhat enlarged. When the patriarchs of our American Church commenced their operations in 1742, they *had* no liturgy with them, as we are informed by the Hallische Nachrichten,* and for ten years they seem to have conducted the services without the book, though probably according to its substance.† In 1785, a

* Hall. Nachrichten, pp. 675, 676.

† Speaking of the Lutheran Church in Europe, Dr. Mosheim says: "Each country has its own *Liturgy*, or form of worship; in accordance with which everything pertaining to public religious exercises and worship must be ordered and performed. These liturgies are frequently enlarged, amended, and explained, as circumstances and occasions demand by the decrees and statutes of the sovereigns."

resolution was passed "That our Directory foı worship should be printed in an altered or enlarged form:" which was published in 1786, and was used for thirty-two years, until another edition was issued by the "Synod of Pennsylvania and adjoining States," in 1818. This was revised and enlarged" by a Committee of the same Synod about fifteen years ago. In the year 1812 the Synod or Ministerium of New York published a "new and enlarged" liturgy in the English language, for the use of its English churches; which was also used by those of other Synods; until the General Synod published an English translation of the Pennsylvania Liturgy, and recommended it to such churches as desired to employ one. But it is worthy of remark, that for

These liturgies in all essential points are substantially alike, though they differ in matters of minor moment.

See Dr. Mosheim's Ecc. Hist. Vol. III. p. 130. Murdock's ed. (Cent. XVI. pt. II. § 5).

But although there is a great diversity of liturgies in the different kingdoms, dukedoms, principalities, and even some individual cities; there is an increasing desire in this country, that the Liturgy of the General Synod, and no other, should be employed in the services of all her churches. We are moreover ourselves of opinion, that the liturgy of our General Synod, moderate in length, solemn and chaste in style, tends to promote uniformity as well as increasing attachment to our beloved Lutheran Zion. Yet should its use be voluntary and not coerced.

more than sixty years past, the liturgy was used almost exclusively by the German churches in Philadelphia, New York, and Baltimore, whilst in the country it was used either not at all, or only on sacramental and festival occasions.

But of late years, an increasing attachment to external ceremonies, and to a uniformity of such external rites and ceremonies, has manifested itself, especially in the German and more symbolic portions of the Church. To a brief liturgy and to simple forms or mode of worship, as above stated, we do not object. Nor do we deprecate argumentative efforts to promote uniformity in these respects; yet as far as these rites are additions to the primitive mode of worship, we decidedly object to all coercion in their adoption. Whilst the use of the liturgy may properly be recommended, its actual employment by every church must be and remain optional. In this position we are fully sustained by the opinion and arguments of the illustrious Reformer himself, whilst those who, on other subjects, so often appeal to his authority are in conflict with him.

"I hold," says Luther, "that it is not advisable to call a convention on the subject of unity in ecclesiastical rites and ceremonies, for it is a thing attended by injurious consequences, even if attempted with an upright zeal. If one Church will not conform to another voluntarily, what need is there of imposing things on the people by the resolutions of councils, which will soon grow into a law, and lay restraint on their souls or consciences. Let one church, therefore, imitate the customs of another voluntarily, or let each church adhere to its own usages: if only unity of spirit be preserved in faith and word, no injury will result from diversity in earthly and visible things (or rites)." *

* Luther's Works, Vol. XVIII. p. 2501. Walch's edit.

CHAPTER XI.

The Distinctive Usages or Denominational Peculiarities of the Church of the General Synod are accordant with Scripture and Scripture Principles.

HESE peculiarities are: 1. The practice of *Catechisation.* 2. *Confirmation.* 3. The observance of the fundamental historical *Festivals* of Christianity; and, 4. Stated *Special Conferences*, for the purpose of spending several days in preaching and other devotional exercises, to awaken and convert sinners and edify believers.

1. By *Catechisation*, we here mean the course of instruction given to catechumens prior to Confirmation. This feature of our system, more than any other, confers efficiency on it, making it missionary and aggressive. It is the secret of our great success in the evangelizing of the masses. It lays hold of the rising generation, and trains it for God and his Church. This feature of our system should be magnified amongst us, and receive the special atten-

tion of ministers, churches, and Synods. Ministers should see to it, that all the children within their pastoral district and charge are brought into the Sabbath School and Bible Classes, and thus trained together as the *children of the Church,* until they are of sufficient age to join the *class of catechumens,* and be prepared for *Confirmation.*

Catechisation of Catechumens and *Confirmation,* though closely connected in our Church and that of the German Reformed, were originally unconnected rites. Catechumens in the earlier ages were adult Heathen or Jews, who having become impressed with the truth and importance of the Christian religion, and willing to adopt it, were received into a class for the purpose of more particular instruction * in the principles of Christian doctrine and practice, at the close of which they made a public profession of religion (that is, were received as full members of the Church) by *baptism;* but were not *confirmed* at all. This catechumenical system, which began in the second century, reached its culmination in the fifth, and ended in the sixth,† chiefly for want of subjects; the great body of heathen and Jews having been received into the Church.

Confirmation, on the other hand, related to those baptized in their *infancy,* and took its rise in the

* Siegel's Handbuch der Ch. Kirchlichen Alterthümer, Vol. I. p. 364, &c.

† *Idem,* p. 372.

second century, when diocesan bishops arose, and claimed the right to sanction or *confirm* (Firmelung —confirmation) the baptisms administered by ordinary ministers. At first this *confirmation* took place at the next visit of the bishop to the church. Afterwards it was separated from baptism, and between the eighth and thirteenth centuries became a distinct ordinance, and was even regarded as a sacrament in the Romish Church. But no instruction was ordinarily given in preparation for it.* Catechetical instruction of the young, in preparation for *Confirmation, is chiefly a Protestant institution*, being a combination of the instruction which had been given chiefly to the Heathen and Jewish adult catechumens, with the rite of Confirmation, which had been a supplement to infant baptism.

Long before the Reformation the Romish Church rigidly required the baptism of all infants, as well as their confirmation at from ten to thirteen years of age, and the civil authorities of Protestant, continental Europe, enforced the same practice. This *Confirmation* of the entire population of the nation so indiscriminately and at so early an age, together with their consequent equally indiscriminate admission to the Lord's Supper, left neither room for the voluntary profession of religion on the ground of

* *Idem*, pp. 446–456. Also Alt's Christlicher Cultus, p. 14.

personal conversion, nor any ordinance of the Church as the badge of such profession. In our happy country where the Church is left free to administer her own affairs, unhampered by the interference of civil government, and among the Dissenters in England, the Protestant Churches have returned to the apostolic method, and insist more on moral qualifications as a prerequisite to a *personal profession* of religion, whether that profession is made in the form of *Confirmation*, or *Adult Baptism*, or *Sacramental Communion.** As the rising generation amongst us, being chiefly the offspring of Christian parents, are (excepting in the Baptist Church) baptized in infancy, by the agency of their parents, it is proper that these subjects of pedobaptism, when arrived at years of maturity, should assume these vows for themselves, and make their profession of religion personally. This public act of personal profession, accompanied by religious exercises, is, in the Lutheran and German Reformed and Protestant Episcopal Churches, styled Confirmation. It is nothing else than *the personal assumption by those baptized in infancy, of the vows made for them by others at their baptism*—a solemn mode of making a profession of religion.

* See the writer's Sermon on the Revival of Religion at Antioch, *Acts* xi. 23, preached at Hanover, 1862, pp. 14, 15.

I. MODE OF CATECHETICAL INSTRUCTION FOR CONFIRMATION.

As these peculiarities of the Lutheran Church, namely, instruction of the Catechetical Class and their Confirmation, are regarded as of the utmost importance to the prosperity of the Church and the salvation of souls, and as we personally consider them as among the chief glories of our Church, we shall present a detailed view of them. This is the more seasonable, as much of the benefit attending it depends on the manner in which the work is done.

Once a year, and as much oftener as circumstances may render proper, it is the custom of Lutheran ministers publicly to appoint a meeting with those persons who have a desire to apply for sacramental privileges. The day selected is usually two or three months prior to the approaching communion season. The persons particularly invited to attend this meeting are, first, those who have been awakened to a sense of their sinfulness and danger, who desire to take up their cross and follow the Redeemer; and, secondly, those who, having been admitted to visible membership in their infancy, have attained the age when it is their duty publicly to profess the religion of Jesus before the church and the world, by *confirming* or taking upon themselves the vows made for them at their baptism in infancy. Prior to this meeting, the pastor endeavors to visit all the awakened souls in his congregation, as also those families in which he knows there are some members of suitable age for sacramental privileges. If, in these visits, the interrogatory be propounded to him by some anxious parent, "What shall I do;—my son, or my daughter, has no desire to meet with you?" We would reply, persuade and require them to attend the instruction; for you are commanded to bring up your offspring in the nurture and admonition of the Lord. But let the minister also distinctly inform the parents and catechumens, and publicly announce it to the congregation, that attendance on this instruction will by no means make it obligatory or even proper for them to approach the sacred board, unless the course of instruction is the means of awakening their souls and leading them to an entire dedication of themselves to God for time and eternity. Nay, according to the Formula of Government and Discipline,* no church council can with propriety admit persons of a different character.

The appointed day finds the pastor and catechumens (for thus are those termed who attend) assembled in the church or lecture-room. Every meeting is opened by singing and prayer, and closed by an address to the throne of grace. The time of the

* Chap. IV. § 5.

first meeting is chiefly occupied by the pastor in explaining the object of the contemplated course of instruction in as solemn and impressive a manner as possible. This object he states to be, *not* merely committing the catechism to memory, or acquiring doctrinal knowledge; for what would all this profit if the heart remained unaffected, the life unchanged? The devils possess more doctrinal knowledge than the most eminent Christians, but remain devils still. Nor is the object contemplated merely admission to the Lord's table. Judas probably reclined with the Master at the sacred board, and yet betrayed him; and Paul tells us that many others ate and drank judgment to themselves. But, says the zealous pastor, who feels the eternal importance of this solemn occasion, The object is to show you, in so plain and simple a manner that you cannot fail to understand it, the natural depravity of your hearts, your habitual and base rebellion against your best benefactor, your Father and your God, and your danger of being shut out forever from his blissful presence: To show you that you must be born again, or be eternally excluded from the kingdom of heaven; and to give you such instructions and directions from day to day as will, if faithfully pursued, sooner or later certainly eventuate in the conversion of your souls to God. Yea, if ye will now but seek the Lord sincerely and perseveringly, ye shall find him; for him that cometh unto him he will in no wise cast out. Further he tells them, if you would seek the Lord aright, you must *surrender your heart* to him; that is, (*a*) form a resolution, that, in the strength of God, you will from this moment indulge in no known sin, and will endeavor to discharge all your known duty. (*b*) Again, when you go hence, meditate much and attentively on the solemn facts you have heard, and examine your heart in regard to them. (*c*) Retire to your closet, or some other suitable place, and with the utmost sincerity pour out your soul in prayer to God. If your heart is cold, and you feel no concern about your salvation, let this very indifference on so momentous a matter be the subject of your confession to God, and beseech him to deliver you from this dangerous condition. (*d*) Resolve that you will continue thus to seek him, by watchfulness, meditation, and frequent prayer; not only daily, so long as the course of instruction continues, but so long as you live; and that if God should suffer your soul to remain in darkness until your final hour, you will die a praying sinner.

The time of every future meeting is taken up partly by plain, practical, conversational lectures, and partly by examinations of the catechumens on the fundamental doctrines of the Scriptures. In the former the pastor passes over, in regular and successive portions, the entire subject of experimental religion, very much after the manner of Doddridge, in his "Rise and Progress of Religion in the Soul;" illustrating the subject by facts drawn from his own experience and observation, and investing it with the utmost possible practical interest by occasional introduction of the peculiar circumstances, temptations, and encouragements of his catechumens. For each such exercise the pious pastor will prepare his own mind by the same devotional exercises of the closet, as for the public duties of the sacred desk. To such deliberate and conscientious preparation he will find himself urged by his annual and accumulating experience, that the good effected by him will be very much graduated by the solemnity and interest which he has brought his own mind to feel on the subject. The writer would here recommend to his younger brethren a practice, on which experience has taught him to place a high value; namely, themselves to read a chapter in that invaluable work of Dr. Doddridge prior to each meeting with their catechumens, and by careful premeditation to prepare themselves for the introduction above referred to, of the peculiar circumstances of those whom they are laboring to conduct to the Redeemer's arms. And having assumed the work of recommendation, he would respectfully submit to his ministerial brethren generally the propriety of enjoining it on all their catechumens acquainted with the English language, to procure and daily to make a faithful use of that excellent little volume, the "Catechumen's and Communicant's Companion," by the Rev. Dr. J. G. Morris.

In the doctrinal instructions, the Scriptures and the Catechism are made the basis, portions of which are committed to memory by those catechumens who are able, on which the pastor makes such explanatory remarks as he deems necessary. Sometimes he calls on one of the catechumens to make the closing prayer, if he regards any of them as spiritually qualified for this duty. Sometimes he may address himself to some individual by name, and hear from him the state of his heart, and his progress in the great work of seeking salvation. Many of our pastors regard it as a duty thus to converse with each catechumen, either in the presence of all, or by daily detailing a few for this purpose, after the others have been dismissed.*

* A similar practice was observed by Dr. Henry Mühlenberg, of Lancaster, as is evident from his letter to his father, in 1785, contained in the *Hallische Nachrichten*, p. 1500: "During the Passion season I also had seventy firstlings (catechumens) attending a course of instruction, of whom five are heads of families. The greater part of them attended in daytime, and six or seven in the evening. My method is this: — I let them commit to memory the Deca-

Such is the course of instruction substantially pursued by the great mass of our divines, with the variations which the habits and predilections of each may dictate, and the exercise of which the principles of Christian liberty, so highly prized and so fully enjoyed in the Lutheran Church, secure to all; yet has it not unfrequently been the theme of invidious clamor to the illiterate enthusiast, and of animadversion from others better informed. But we have never heard, nor do we expect ever to hear, of a single truly pious pastor, who faithfully attended to this instruction, and did not regard it as a highly blessed means of bringing souls to Christ. By unconverted ministers this duty, like all others, will be performed as a mere formality, and confer little

logue, the [Apostles'] Creed, the Lord's Prayer, the principal Scripture passages concerning Baptism and the Lord's Supper, and the Creed in a hymn, [by the Court preacher, Ziegenhagen,] and then take them through a course of Christian doctrine. In the latter part of the course I *each day examine ten or twelve of them separately*, presenting to them upwards of thirty essential questions. Afterwards I *keep them back* [after the balance are dismissed], and explain to them more fully the vows they are to take, and let them make the promise *individually to me*, and then I *pray with them.* Thus I am certain that *each one* is sufficiently instructed, and there is this gain, that my catechumens have confidential intercourse with me, and entertain childlike and fraternal affection for me."

benefit on those who attend on it. But in the hands of the great mass of our pastors it is nothing else than a series of meetings for prayer, singing, exhortation, and individual personal interview between them and those who profess a concern for salvation; in which, without adopting the novel nomenclature of the day, they can enjoy all the facilities and afford to their hearers all the benefits aimed at, and doubtless often attained by others, in what are termed anxious meetings, inquiry meetings, class meetings, private conferences, &c. &c. Indeed, the friends of this good old custom are delighted to see the several sister denominations, under different appellations, adopting the substance of the same thing; nor do we care by what name the thing is known, so that God is glorified and sinners are saved.

THE VOTE OF THE CHURCH COUNCIL.

When this course of instruction has been concluded, the church council is invited to attend with the pastor on an appointed day, for the purpose of examining the applicants for sacramental communion, and either admitting or rejecting them. This meeting has usually been held in the church, in the presence of the whole congregation; but such entire publicity is unfavorable to free and confidential interview with the catechumens, and has in many cases converted this exercise into a mere general examination on the doctrines and duties of the Christian religion. The writer cannot refrain from expressing his decided preference for the practice of those brethren who hold this final meeting in the lecture-room or school-house, in the presence of the church council alone, and there enter into an individual and personal examination of the applicants on the momentous subject of their own evidences of personal piety. Such is manifestly the nature of the duty contemplated by our Formula of Church Government, Chap. IV. § 5:—

"It shall be the duty of the council to admit to membership, adults who make application, and whom, *on mature examination*, they shall judge to be possessed of the qualifications hereafter specified. They shall be obedient subjects of Divine grace; that is, they must either be genuine Christians, or satisfy the church council that they are sincerely endeavoring to become such; that is, they must satisfy the church council that they have faithfully performed all that is in their power, in order to accomplish this end. In the language of systematic theology, they must have done all that is *voluntary* in the great work of conversion. Conversion, or repentance in a general sense, may be viewed in a twofold light, as *active* and as *passive.* The former includes all that the repenting sinner himself is required to do; and the latter embraces that influence which God exerts on the mind and heart of the sinner during the progress of this change. The church council should in all cases require *evidence of those changes and acts which constitute genuine conversion in the active or voluntary sense of the term.*

"Conversion or regeneration, as far as known to us, consists in a radical change of the religious views, feelings, purposes, and habits of action, by which the sinner becomes a new creature in Christ Jesus, which is wrought by the Spirit of God through the truth, by an inward influence on the soul, which is not intelligible to us, but whose certainty is evinced by its results. 'The wind bloweth where it listeth, and thou hearest the sound thereof, but canst not tell whence it cometh, and whither it goeth: *so is every one that is born of the Spirit.*'

"It is also the duty of the council to admit to communion of the church, all those who were admitted to church-membership in their infancy, and whom, *on like examination,* they shall judge possessed of the above-mentioned qualifications. No one shall be considered a fit subject for confirmation who has not previously attended a course of religious lectures, delivered by the pastor on the most important doctrines and principles of religion; unless the pastor should be satisfied that the applicant's attainments are adequate without this attendance."

How can the requisitions of this clause be considered as satisfied by a general examination of the catechumens, on the attainments they have made in the knowledge of Christian doctrine and duties?

II. CONFIRMATION, OR PUBLIC PROFESSION OF RELIGION BEFORE THE WHOLE CHURCH.

After the examination of applicants has been closed, and their cases decided by the council, those who have been admitted are required to make a public profession of the religion of Jesus Christ before the whole church, by *confirming,* or taking on themselves the vows of dedication to God, made for them at their baptism in infancy.

Should there be among the catechumens any who had not been baptized in infancy, they are required to make precisely the same public profession as a prerequisite to their baptism, which is performed prior to the confirmation of the others. And as this profession is thus, in the first instance, made by themselves, and in adult age, the *confirmation* or personal assumption of it by them would seem to be superfluous, although no perceptible evil could result from their being *confirmed* along with the rest, as has in some few instances been done.

After the catechumens have made the public profession of the religion of Christ, they all kneel around the altar, when the minister implores upon them the blessings of God, in a brief ejaculatory prayer, passing from one to the other, and successively imposing his hands on the head of each.

The imposition of hands, although generally practised, is not regarded by us as an essential part of this public ceremony, nor do we attribute to the whole ordinance any other than a moral influence.

It is this public profession of religion and the blessing of God pronounced on the subject, to which specifically the name of *Confirmation* is now given; because the catechumen literally *confirms* the vows made for him in his infancy. *Confirmation,* among us, *may* therefore *be defined, a solemn mode of admitting to sacramental communion, those who had been admitted to church-membership by baptism in their infancy.* What we regard as essential in it, is practised by all Christian denominations which require a profession of religion before admission to sacramental communion. The circumstances peculiar to us, viz., the antecedent course of instruction, the *public* profession before the whole congregation, and the individual prayer of the pastor with his hand on the head of each catechumen, experience has taught us to regard as happily calculated to heighten the intense solemnity of the occasion, and fix on the heart of each individual the indelible impression that he is now consecrated to God, whilst they are all perfectly consonant with the spirit of the Gospel, and sanctioned by the example of the earlier ages of the Christian Church.

As to the *public* profession of religion before the whole church, instead of before the church council or session, though it may require more self-denial, it certainly tends to impress more deeply the mind of the catechumen himself, whilst it draws the line of distinction more clearly between him and the world.

This rite has sometimes been considered as a continuation of a practice somewhat similar, of which a few cases are related in Scripture.* It is indeed

* *Acts* viii. 14–17: "When the apostles, who were at Jerusalem, heard that Samaria had received the word of God, they sent unto them Peter and John: who, when they were come down, prayed for them that they might receive the Holy Ghost. For as yet, he was fallen upon none of them; only they were baptized in the name of the Lord Jesus. *Then laid they their hands on them, and they received the Holy Ghost.*" *Acts* xix. 1–6: "And it came to pass, that while Apollos was at Corinth, Paul, having passed through the upper coasts, came to Ephesus. And finding certain disciples, he said unto them, Have ye received the Holy Ghost since ye believed? And they said unto him, We have not so much as heard whether there be any Holy Ghost. And he said unto them, Unto what then were ye baptized? And they said, Unto John's baptism. Then said Paul, John verily baptized with the baptism of repentance, saying unto the people that they should believe on him that should come after him, that is on Jesus the Messiah. When they heard this they were baptized in the name of the Lord Jesus.

evident, that the design and effect of the imposition of hands, described in the annexed passages, was the communication of miraculous gifts, which have confessedly long since ceased. But there is another passage,* in which the Apostle Paul speaks of "laying on of the hands" as among the "principles," or elementary things, belonging to Christianity. And as no other rite has descended from the apostolic Church, to which the apostle could possibly allude, it is inferred by some, that although the imposition of hands was first designed to confer the extraordinary gifts of the Holy Ghost, it was continued after those miraculous powers had ceased, as a suitable mode of imploring the divine blessing on those who were to be admitted to the sacred board. The Apology to the Augsburg Confession contains the following declaration on this subject: *Confirmation is a rite which was transmitted to us from the fathers, but which the Church never regarded as essential to*

And when Paul *laid his hands upon them,* the Holy Ghost came on them, and they spake with tongues and prophesied."

* *Heb.* vi. 1, 2: "Therefore leaving (της ἀρχῆς) the first principles or the elements of the doctrine of Christ, let us go on unto perfection; not laying again the foundation concerning repentance from dead works, and faith towards God, concerning the doctrine of baptisms, and *the laying on of hands,* and the resurrection of the dead and eternal judgment."

*salvation; for it is not supported by a divine command.** The illustrious Calvin was also favorable to this rite, although his followers in this country seem differently inclined. "It was," says he,† "an ancient custom, that the children of Christian parents, when they were grown up, should be presented to the bishop, to do that office which was required of persons who were baptized at adult age. Forasmuch as that, being baptized in infancy, they could not then make any confession of their faith before the church, they were again brought by their parents before the bishop, and examined by him in the catechism, which they had then in a certain form of words. And that this act, which ought to be grave and sacred, might have the greater reverence, the ceremony of the imposition of hands was used in the exercise of it. So the youth, after their faith was approved, were dismissed with a solemn benediction." Soon after he adds: "Such an imposition of hands as this, which is used purely as a blessing, *I very much approve of, and wish it were now restored to its pure and primitive uses.*" Commenting on the

* Confirmatio (et extrema unctio) sunt ritus accepti a Patribus, quos ne ecclesia quidem tanquam necessarios ad salutem requirit, quia non habent mandatum Dei. — *Apol. to Confession*, Art. XIII. (VII.) p. 203 of Müller's Symbolische Bücher.

† Institutes, lib. iv. c. 1.

passage in Hebrews above referred to, "he considers it as abundantly proving that the origin of Confirmation was from the Apostles," meaning, as we learn from the context of the above quotations, not that it was commanded by the Apostles as a perpetual rite, but merely that it originated in their practice of the imposition of hands.*

There is certainly nothing in the nature of Confirmation itself which was designed to make its subjects members of one particular denomination rather than of another; for, at the time of its introduction, the Christian Church had not yet been divided into different sects on the ground of doctrinal diversity. And it is obvious that baptism made its subject a member of the particular church of that town or place in which he was baptized, and that subsequently his membership in any particular church was decided by his habitual attendance and worship with it. Children were always numbered with that church in which their parents, sponsors, or those with whom they lived, worshipped. Yet Confirmation may very aptly now be regarded as implying the preference of its subject for the particular denomination in which he receives the rite and makes the profession; although, on strict principles of Scriptural church government, his actual member-

* White's Lectures, pp. 140, 141.

ship in any church must be decided by the same circumstances now as in the days of the Apostles.

III. THE OBSERVANCE OF THE FUNDAMENTAL HISTORICAL FESTIVALS OF CHRISTIANITY.

The observance of these festivals is founded on one of the most obvious principles of human nature, the propriety of cherishing the recollection of illustrious deeds and salutary events. This principle has been acted on by nations ancient and modern, as also by the Church of Christ in all ages. Christianity is a religion based upon facts, and designed for all mankind. Now, matters of fact, the truth of which depends on the testimony of the senses, are most easily intelligible to the great body of men, and for obvious reasons arising from the structure of the mind, best calculated to make a deep impression on them. Hence, the very pillars on which Christianity was made to rest, are matters of fact, intelligible in every language, suited to the capacity of every nation, and equally applicable to all future generations, such as the birth, life, miracles, crucifixion, death, resurrection, and ascension of the Saviour. Without admitting the historical reality of these events, no man can be a true Christian, and a sincere and cordial belief of their truth is closely connected with the character of a true disciple of our Lord. Hence all rational means actually tending to extend and perpetuate the knowledge of these facts must exert a salutary influence on Christianity itself. The disorders and dissipation which in some places disgrace these days are remnants of papal corruption, and have no more connection with the rational observance of these festivals than with a fast-day appointed by any church, or by the civil authorities of our land.

Our fathers, in the Reformation of the 16th century, rejected the great majority of the festivals which had accumulated during a thousand years in the Romish Church. But in this country, we observe scarce the half even of those retained in Europe.

The general practice of the churches of the General Synod is embodied in a resolution passed by that body, on the motion of the present writer, at the meeting in Reading, in 1857, (p. 32,) viz:—

"*Resolved,* That the churches in connection with the General Synod be recommended to observe our regular ecclesiastical festivals, in commemoration of the fundamental facts of our religion; viz.: Christmas, Good Friday, Easter, Ascension Day, and Whitsunday, in the hope and persuasion that, by the Divine blessing, they will be found to be, as they have often proved, occasions of reviving our congregations."

The practice has been permitted to pass into desuetude, especially in some of our English congregations, and the design of this resolution was alike to fix the number of these religious festivals, and to encourage their proper religious observance in all our churches.

IV. THE HOLDING OF "SPECIAL CONFERENCES," OR PROTRACTED MEETINGS FOR CONTINUED PREACHING AND OTHER DEVOTIONAL EXERCISES.

In the apostolic age, continued meetings for preaching were not unusual.

"I was DAILY with you in the temple teaching, (that is,) preaching," said the *blessed Saviour* to the multitude, who followed him into the garden of Gethsemane, with swords and staves to take him, (*Mark* xiv. 49.) And again says *Luke*, (xix. 47,) "He (Jesus) taught, (that is,) preached daily in the temple."

The *Apostle Paul* continued preaching at Troas "*until midnight*," when the young man Eutychus, having fallen into a deep sleep, fell down from the third loft, and was taken up dead. And after Paul had gone down, and restored him to life, he continued discoursing to them a long while, "*until break of day*."—*Acts* xx. 7–11.

"And *the believers* (the first converts,) continued to meet *daily* with one accord in the temple; and the Lord added to the church *daily* such as should be saved," (or rather, σωζομενυς, the saved; those that were saved from an ungodly world, or from the dominion and curse of sin.)

Thus we perceive that under the ministry of the Saviour and his apostles, meetings for preaching and prayer were continued *daily* for a length of time. Nor was the continuance of each meeting limited to *one* or *two hours*. In short, the length of the services at each meeting, as well as the continuance of the meetings themselves, were regulated by circumstances of each occasion.

In like manner, at the present day, whilst religious meetings should ordinarily be of moderate length, and convenient frequency, they may with propriety be continued longer and be repeated more frequently on special occasions, when the Holy Spirit is hovering over a congregation, and both saints and sinners feel moved to wrestle with God for a special blessing.

But as the age of the apostles receded, the arrangements for public worship tended toward a stereotyped uniformity, especially after the union of Church and State, by which the civil officers participated in the regulation of ecclesiastical affairs. On the continent of Europe, preaching is, with some exceptions, confined to the Lord's day and festivals, whilst protracted meetings, in the sense of our Special Conferences, are unknown. In this country, such meetings are held by various other denominations, as well as by the churches of the General Synod. Yet their observance, though recommended, is left optional with the individual churches and pastors.

Experience has rendered these meetings increasingly popular, and we anticipate the day with pleasure, when they will be generally attended to. The provisions of the Formula on this subject read as follows: —

Special Conferences.

Chapter XVI. of the Constitution for District Synods: —

Sec. 1. It is earnestly recommended that each Synod divide itself into two or more districts, for the purpose of holding Special Conferences, which may be held either on a weekday or Sabbath.

Sec. 2. It is desirable, when ministers do not live too far apart, that at least two Conferences should be held annually in each district. They ought to last two days, and the chief business to be performed at them is to awaken and convert sinners, and to edify believers by close practical preaching of the gospel.

Sec. 3. The state of religion in the churches of the district ought to be inquired into, and at least an hour be spent by the Conference alone in conversation on subjects relating to pastoral experience.

Sec. 4. These districts ought to contain between five and ten ministers, and when the number becomes greater, a new district ought to be formed.

Sec. 5. These Conferences ought to be held alternately, in some congregation of each minister and licentiate belonging to the district.

Sec. 6. Special Conferences may examine into any business of congregations, which is regularly referred to them, and give their advice; but no Conference shall, under any pretext whatever, perform any business connected with the licensure or ordination of candidates for the ministry.

Sec. 7. Lay delegates may also be sent to these Conferences, under the same regulations as to Synods, if it is thought advisable by the Synod.

The *order*, which it is designed shall be observed at all meetings for public worship, and especially at Special Conferences and prayer-meetings, is in strict accordance with Scripture, and thus defined in our Formula for government and discipline, Chapter VII.

Of Prayer-Meetings, &c.

Sec. 1. As Prayer is one of the most necessary duties of a Christian,* and as prayer-meetings have been of the utmost importance and usefulness, it is therefore most earnestly recommended to the dif-

* Thess. v. 17. "Pray without ceasing."

Luke xviii. 1. "And he spake a parable unto them to this end, that men ought always to pray, and not to faint."

Col. iv. 2. "Continue in prayer, and watch in the same with thanksgiving," &c.

ferent churches in our connection, to establish and promote them among our members. These meetings may be held in the church, school-house, or in private houses, and their object is the spiritual edification of the persons present; but the *utmost precaution must ever be observed, that God, who is a Spirit, be worshipped in spirit and in truth,*—that they be characterized by that solemnity and decorum which ought ever to attend divine worship; and that no disorder be tolerated, or anything that is calculated to interrupt the devotions of those who are convened, or prevent their giving the fullest attention to him who is engaged in leading the meeting,—in short, that, according to the injunctions of the Apostle, *all things be done "decently and in order."*

SEC. 2. It is solemnly recommended to all church-members, and more especially to the members of the council, to make daily worship in their family a sacred duty.*

* Gal. vi. 4. "And ye fathers, provoke not your children to wrath; but bring them up in the nurture and admonition of the Lord."

Acts x. 24. "And the morrow after they (Peter and the brethren) entered into Cesarea. And Cornelius waited for them, and had called together his kinsmen and near friends.—33. Immediately therefore I sent to thee: and thou hast well done that thou art come. Now therefore are *we all here present* before God, to hear all things that are commanded thee of God."

The advantages of Special Conferences are various, and beneficial alike to the ministers and people. They afford ministers more frequent opportunity for social intercourse, and the cultivation of personal friendships, for mutual consultation on their individual pastoral difficulties and successes, and for deliberation on measures for the promotion of the welfare of our churches generally. To church-members, and to the world at large, they afford precious reasons for the conversion of sinners and edification of believers. The Saviour has promised to be with us wherever two or three are assembled in his name. And, doubtless, any special earnestness and special effort on the part of sinners or of saints to seek his favor will be met by the Friend of sinners with a special blessing. It is, moreover, a dictate of common sense, as well as of the laws of our mental organism, that if one sermon, attentively heard, makes some impression on the mind,—listening to two, or three, or more, with little interruption, except by singing and prayer, will deepen the impression. The mind, moreover, not being diverted by intervening days of secular business, will be more readily brought to a stand, and induced to

Isa. x. 25. "Pour out thy fury upon the heathen that know thee not, and upon *the families* that call not on thy name." See Acts ii. 14.

declare for God by the cumulative influence of many consecutive religious exercises, than by one, or than by the same number of detached sermons, where the effect of each one is dissipated by intervening weeks of worldly occupations before the other is heard.

Another object of these special conferences or protracted meetings is to *elevate the standard of piety,* and teach it especially as a matter of *personal experience* and of personal *assurance.* It was in this light that the illustrious Reformer himself regarded and experienced religion. Hear his own words: "Though as a monk I was holy and irreproachable," says he, "my conscience was still filled with troubles and torment. I could not endure the expression, 'the righteous justice of God!' I did not love that just and holy Being who punishes sinners. I felt a secret anger against him. I hated him, because, not satisfied with terrifying by his law, and by the miseries of life, poor creatures already ruined by original sin, he aggravated our suffering by the gospel. But when, by the Spirit of God, I understood these words,—when I learned how the justification of the sinner proceeds from God's mere mercy, by the way of faith,—then *I* FELT *myself born again* as a *new man,* and I entered by an open door *into the very Paradise of God.**

* "Hic me prorsus renatum esse sensi et apertis portis in ipsum Paradisum intrasse."

"From that hour I saw the precious and holy Scriptures with *new eyes.* I went through the whole Bible. I collected a multitude of passages, which taught me what the work of God was. And as I had before heartily hated that expression, 'the righteousness of God,' I began from that time *to value and to love it,* as the sweetest and most consolatory truth. Truly this text of St. Paul was to me the very gate of heaven."

It is worthy of note, that it was whilst hearing Luther's Preface to his Commentary on the Romans read, that the distinguished man of God, *John Wesley,* also learned the nature and experienced the power of this truth. Whilst inquiring after God, he one evening attended a meeting, where a person was reading Luther's Preface to the Epistle to the Romans, and the following are his own words as to the result: "About a quarter before nine," says he, "while he (Luther) was describing the *change which God works in the heart,* through faith in Christ, *I felt my heart strangely warmed. I felt I did trust in Christ,* in Christ alone, for salvation, and *an assurance was given me that he had taken away my sins,*—even mine—and saved me from the law of sin and death. I began to pray with all my might, for those who had in a more especial manner despitefully used me and persecuted me. I then testified openly to all there, *what I now first felt* in my heart."

Here, then, we see, not only that Luther believed in an inward change of heart, or *conversion,* but that he also professed to have experienced it, and to know the exact time when this gracious change occurred within him. How far have those followers of Luther *fallen* from his standard of piety, who ignore the importance of an *internal change of heart,* who disparage the internal *consciousness and assurance* of such a change, and pronounce this view of the testimony of the Spirit to be nothing but fanaticism!

CHAPTER XII.

The Design and Spirit of the General Synod are Scriptural.

IN contemplating the design of the General Synod, it is necessary to revert to the first principles of ecclesiastical organization. We must remember that both our Synods and General Synod, as well as Presbyterian Synods and General Assembly, the Episcopal Convention, and the Methodist General Conference, are all *voluntary associations.* They are confessedly not sustained by an exact example of any such institution in the New Testament. But they are authorized by the principle involved in the meeting of the Apostles, elders, and brethren convened at Jerusalem, and recorded in the 15th chapter of the Acts of the Apostles. They are legitimate developments of that principle — that is, applications of it — to the peculiar circumstances and necessities of the Church in different ages, and among different people. All ecclesiastical associations, beyond the independent congregation of the New Testament, are of this voluntary kind. It is an erroneous idea, that Synods possess any inherent powers from God, beyond what is delegated to them by the churches, for they are not even mentioned in His Word. And in the Lutheran churches of Germany, Sweden and Denmark, there were no Synods during the first three centuries of their history. Synods can possess only those powers delegated to them by the individual ministers and congregations by which they are formed, and the General Synod only such as are delegated to it by the District Synods. Of course, after these powers have been delegated to a higher judicatory thus formed, they cannot be exercised by the lower body during its connection with the higher. The nature and extent of these powers are defined in the constitutions of these bodies, and their general design is ordinarily announced in the preamble to it.

In regard to the Design and Spirit of the Church of the Redeemer in general, there can be no doubt. The final commission of the Saviour evinces it to be a missionary organization, a progressive institution, destined to pass the boundaries of Judea, and to fill the world with a knowledge of the truth as it is in Jesus.

"Go ye," said the Divine Master to his disciples, "and preach the gospel to every creature." "Go ye and make disciples (μαϑητευσατε, from μαϑητης, a disciple) of all nations, baptizing them in the name of the Father and of the Son and of the Holy Ghost; and lo! I am," &c. The Church of Christ was instituted not for the conversion and salvation of the Jews only, but also of the Gentiles — and not of any one Gentile nation alone, but of all nations. The grand aim of the Church ought to be such, in her organization and measures, as to promote most successfully the conversion of the whole world. "The field," said the Saviour, "is the world;" and for any Church to lose sight of this is to turn recreant to the cause of our Divine Master. The work of the minister was not to attack and battle the subtleties of Pagan philosophy, but to assail and grapple with the palpable immoralities and practical infidelity of mankind. The Church ought to adopt such a system as not, by its particularity, to split up the body of Christ, and exclude a large portion of the best, the most spiritual and active Christians from her communion; for this fritters away her energies, intellectual and pecuniary, and thus retards her progress. She should also avail herself of all the increasing light and knowledge and improvements of sciences which God in his providence places in her reach.

Now this is exactly the object for which our Lutheran General Synod was designed. It originated from fraternal regard and love to the Lutheran name and principles among men who differed amongst themselves even on some important doctrines of Christianity; for it cannot be denied that the older and larger Synods, which aided in forming the General Synod, embraced some grave errorists in their membership, though they were not generally the active friends of this body. Hence it was made a loose confederacy of independent bodies, which reserved all the natural powers of Churches and Synods, except such as were expressly delegated in the constitution.

After several of these District Synods had seceded from the General Synod, its remaining constituency was in favor of a closer union and a more definite avowal of the grand doctrines of the gospel. The aim was to exclude all fundamental errorists, and open the door for all pious Lutherans of the different minor shades of doctrinal views, *who possessed liberality and charity enough to co-operate with their brethren, and to concede to them the liberty of diversity in minor points which they ask for themselves. No others were invited.* The wisdom of the course pursued by the General Synod is very evident.

If we make *all the minor points symbolical,* many of those born in the Lutheran Church are compelled to leave it, and do leave it, as they grow up and think for themselves; and few from without will seek admission into our communion.

If we adhere to the General Synod's basis of Augsburg Confession alone, all can remain, and many will join us from without.

Churches confining their creed to the more important doctrines, will *rarely, if ever*, find any occasion *to change them;* for whilst there is no end to the fluctuations and vagaries of unconverted intellects, the great body of regenerate minds have always found what are called the *fundamental* or cardinal doctrines in the Bible as to all their essential features.

Churches making many minor and less certain doctrines symbolical, will always find many born in their pale unable to believe some of these doctrines, who will often cause strife, and endeavor to change their symbol.

As the Scriptures give us no injunction to form human creeds and to bind the consciences of men, we have no authority to advance any farther in this work, or to require unity in more doctrines than are necessary to harmonious co-operation; not among bigots, but among enlightened Christians.

The General Synod has therefore done wisely in adopting a basis requiring only the profession, "that we believe the Augsburg Confession to be a correct exhibition of the *fundamental* doctrines of the Scriptures," thus leaving the conscience of its churches free in regard to all non-fundamental doctrines, and every non-fundamental phase or circumstance connected with the fundamental doctrines themselves.

The General Synod was never intended to do the work of District Synods, except in a few cases of appeal, for the promotion of concord and settlement of disputes. No ; it is designed to occupy *a higher standpoint* than the District Synods. These are mainly *business Associations*, to transact the current affairs of the churches connected with them, and requiring combined counsel and action. But the General Synod is designed to review the progress and operations of the District Synods, to harmonize their influence on each other, to prevent and remove friction, to deliberate on the interests of the whole Church and give them the highest efficiency. All this it does from the Saviour's exalted standpoint, "*The* field is the world." She is to contemplate the influence of other denominations on us, and our influence on them; and to endeavor to prevent denominational interference in the sublime work of subduing the world unto Christ, and to develop the Lutheran Church as nearly as possible on apostolic principles.

But as to the design of the General Synod, let us listen to her constitution, and be instructed by herself.

1. The *first* object or design of the General Synod

was to promote Christian union among the different portions of our Church, and among all denominations of Christians in general. The preamble to the Constitution defines the object of the body as being "For the promotion of the practice of brotherly love, to the furtherance of Christian concord, and to the firm establishment and continuance of the unity of the Spirit in the bond of peace," &c. And in Art. III. Sect. VIII. of the original Constitution (adopted in 1820), we read these truly apostolic words: "The General Synod shall apply all their powers, their prayers, and their means toward the prevention of schisms amongst us, and be sedulously and incessantly regardful of the circumstances of the times, and of every casual rise and progress of unity of sentiment among *Christians in general, of whatever kind or denomination*, in order that the blessed opportunities to heal the wounds and schisms already existing in the Church of Christ, and to promote concord and unity, may not pass by neglected and unavailing."

The Church of Christ is, and ever must be, *essentially one.* Its members in different denominations may differ in forms of worship, in discipline and government; but they are one in essential doctrine, one in the manifestations of Christian life, and one in mutual and *universal* love. That religion which enables us to love those we have never seen, must be more than human; it is not of earth, but of heaven. In the progress of the Church's history and development, diversities of circumstances and condition have arisen, tending to alienate the affection of those whom Christ designed to be one. But the knowledge of this design, "that all should be one as he and the Father are one," as well as the essential nature of all true religion, which is love, makes it the duty of all Christians of every name to promote unity and brotherly affection among all who name the name of Christ, and aspire to the exalted character of Christians on earth, and fellow-citizens with the saints in heaven.

This high obligation the enlightened founders of our General Synod duly appreciated and fully expressed in the clauses of her Constitution above cited. Let us, therefore, as faithful sons of this noble institution, ever prove ourselves the enlightened advocates of every judicious effort to accelerate the fulfilment of the Saviour's aspiration. Thirty years ago, the present writer published an Appeal on this subject to the Christian public, with a new "Plan for *Catholic Union on Apostolic Principles,*" which seemed to commend itself to the judgment of the Protestant denominations of our land very extensively. But a variety of circumstances combined to divert public attention from the subject, and to retard the progress of its adoption. The subject has of late been receiving renewed attention, and possibly something effectual may yet be accomplished.

Yet are there certain essential and indispensable prerequisites to Christian union, in the absence of which the attempt to unite different Christians into one body must necessarily prove abortive, and tend to make the Church of God still more a Babel of jarring tongues and of endless strife. These conditions are: *first,* actual *agreement* in those *doctrines* termed *fundamental,* and deemed necessary to salvation by all Evangelical denominations. *Secondly,* there must also exist sincere charity and toleration of each other's non-fundamental differences of doctrine and mode of worship; and, *thirdly,* absence of opposite and conflicting modes of government or ritual, such as diocesan episcopacy and parity.

When the several District Synods of the Lutheran Church organized the General Synod in 1820, these three conditions were present, and the union was a cordial one. They all held the fundamental doctrines; and although there existed non-fundamental differences, they had *charity* towards each other. Accordingly the union was productive of the greatest advantages. But after the recession of the Pennsylvania Synod from that body in 1823, on account of some misapprehensions and popular clamor against the General Synod, Bible Societies,

&c., by their laity, they, during the thirty years of their separation, not only changed some of their doctrinal views on minor points, and became rigidly symbolic, but they also degenerated into bigotry and intolerance. Hence, ever since their reunion with the General Synod in 1853, they have been denouncing the other Synods in the connection for not adhering rigidly to the Confessions of the 16th century, and for holding the same views formerly professed by the greater part of themselves. As they were constantly laboring for the restorations of those obsolete ideas, and of course were opposed by the other Synods, they were the cause of frequent controversies in the Church. Being destitute of the second prerequisite for union, namely, cordial charity and toleration, a willingness, with the noble Apostle Paul, "to receive a brother that is weak in the faith, but not for doubtful disputation," they were no longer morally qualified for the union, and their continuance in the General Synod could be productive of no good. Whilst, therefore, we deplored their want of charity, which disqualified them for union, we regard it as more honorable to themselves, and more conducive to the prosperity of all parties, to withdraw from the General Synod, than to remain, and by continuing to cause constant contentions, divert the attention and energies of the Synod from the more important practical objects enjoined on the Church by the Saviour. These views we repeatedly expressed at the late meeting of the General Synod at Fort Wayne, both publicly and in private, to some leading members of the opposition, before their withdrawal. Probably, after a quarter of a century expended in the vain attempt to make *even their own members* think alike on all minor topics, they will be constrained by an increase of Christian charity and experience, as well as of love to the Saviour's prayer, to return and propose a reunion with their former brethren, and doubtless be cordially received.

This was a union of Lutheran Synods with a Lutheran General Synod; but the union of the several leading Protestant denominations into one ecclesiastical body, is a somewhat different problem. There are indeed some minor denominations which differ so little from others, that, if they abounded in Christian charity or love, they could advantageously be united to their larger homogeneous neighbors. Thus the different bodies of Presbyterians, Old and New School, Seceders, Cumberland Presbyterians, &c., and the different classes of Methodists, Old School, the Protestant Methodists, the United Brethren, &c., we think might ultimately be amalgamated with advantage to the common cause. But that a *Confederation,* and not an Amalgamation of the leading Protestant denominations of our land, is desirable, is evident. The whole body of Protestants united into one close organization, would be too unwieldy for practical purposes; unless it could be subdivided geographically, as the churches in the earlier ages were. All that seems to be feasible or desirable, is: 1. The union of the several homogeneous sects, which differ in little else than the name. And, 2. More spiritual union, Christian love and fellowship between the several leading denominations, by the establishment of such bonds of fraternal recognition, by occasional sacramental and ministerial communion, by the adoption of such principles of co-operation and non-interference as would tend to form a *Confederation,* and not an amalgamation of the different parts of the Protestant world, on the principles laid down in our Fraternal Appeal to the Protestant Churches, published in 1838. Such a union leaving to each denomination the ultimate control of its own affairs, we feel confident, would accomplish the prayer of the blessed Saviour, would greatly promote peace and brotherly love throughout the Churches, and hasten the spread of the gospel over the entire globe. But as this plan cannot be fully adopted at once, let all denominations, which are not already doing so, begin by practising free sacramental communion, giving an invitation to all members of other Churches in good standing, who may be present, to unite with them in the Holy

Supper; by an occasional interchange of pulpits, to publish their mutual recognition of ministerial character; by co-operation in objects of catholic nature and of common interest, such as Bible, Tract, and some other Societies. Thus would union of spirit precede unity of external organizations, and prepare the way for as near an external union as the Saviour designed, and as experience would prove to be useful. Thus would we soon realize the vision of the prophet: "Thy watchmen shall lift up the voice; with the voice together shall they sing: for they shall see eye to eye, when the Lord shall bring again Zion:" (*Is.* lii. 8;) and also that of the psalmist: "Behold how good and how pleasant it is for brethren to dwell together in unity! It is like the precious ointment on the head, that ran down upon the beard, even Aaron's beard, that went down to the skirts of his garment." (*Ps.* cxxxiii. 1.)

Another object of the friends of General Synod *originally* was to entrust to that body the exclusive right to propose and publish books for public use in the churches, as was explicitly stated in the *Plan-Entwurf*, or outlines of a plan for the Central Union of the Evangelical Lutheran Church in the United States, out of which the Constitution of the General Synod grew.

A *third* design of the General Synod was to promote theological education, and elevate the standard of education in general amongst ministers, and also to increase their numbers. In Art. III. Sect. VI. we are told: "The General Synod may devise plans for Seminaries of Education, and Missionary Institutions, as well as for the aid of poor ministers and their widows, and orphans of ministers, and endeavor, with the help of God, to carry them into effect." There is a peculiar propriety in the General Synod devoting special attention to ministerial education, as the mother Church in Germany was always distinguished for her eminence in learning.

Here we also have the cause of *Missions* avowed as the *fourth* object;

And the *Aid and Support of poor ministers and their widows and orphans* as the *Fifth* design of the General Synod.

These objects are of so high and noble a character, that too much cannot be said in commendation of their intrinsic dignity and excellence, or of their far-reaching and salutary influence; but the limits prescribed for this work do not admit of their further discussion.

In conclusion, we perceive that the General Synod of the Evangelical Lutheran Church in the United States is a peculiar, a noble, and most elevated institution, standing in advance of all the other denominational organizations of the day, contending for the acknowledged "faith once delivered to the saints;" but not for the doubtful disputations and additions of men,—regarding the extended symbols of the sixteenth century as human and fallible productions, though useful books of study, and binding on the consciences of men only the fundamental doctrines of Scripture, as taught in the ecumenical creeds of the earlier ages, and in the Augsburg Confession. We find, that in accordance with the apostolic injunction to the Romans, this noble body "receives into its embrace the brother who is weak in the faith, but not for doubtful disputation."

This body raises no walls of partition between the disciples of the Divine Master; but receives all who love the Lord Jesus Christ in sincerity, who believe the acknowledged "faith once delivered to the saints," the common doctrines of the Reformation, the grand fundamental truths of the *Gospel*, and who prefer the mode of worship and other peculiarities of the churches of the Evangelical Lutheran General Synod.

This body freely allows diversity of views on points of non-fundamental character, which do not interfere with harmonious co-operation in the same church, *and invites none into her connection, who do not approve of this toleration.* But it requires, and must necessarily demand, of those desiring to enter it, that they exercise the same charity toward their brethren which these extend to them, and that they abstain from all *personal* and *criminative* controversy on these non-essential topics. Controversy by Christians should never be personal, and should more generally consist in defences of the *acknowledged* doctrines and institutions of the Church against an ungodly and unbelieving world. Discussions *between* Christians must, of course, relate to non-fundamental points, and should always be conducted in the spirit of brotherly love, whilst truth, and not victory, should be the constant aim of all parties.

Again, we have seen that the grand objects contemplated by the General Synod partake of the moral sublime. That noble institution stands on no sectarian basis, but rises to the standpoint of Christ and his Apostles. *Her "field is the world,"* and her directory for its cultivation is the unadulterated, inspired Word of God. She gratefully accepts whatever providential light is afforded in the developments of her history, through those honored instrumentalities which the Master has employed, such as an Augustine, a Wickliffe, a Huss, a Jerome, a Luther, a Melanchthon, a Calvin, a Zwingli, a Wesley, and others; but she keeps her eye steadily fixed *above them on the Master*, and cherishes her constant paramount obligation to the inspired directions which He left, and to the constant guidance of that Spirit who was promised "to lead her children into all necessary truth."

All those institutions or instrumentalities which God has especially blessed for the advancement of his Church, and which are judged accordant with the principles of his Word, the General Synod, by a careful, judicious exercise of judgment, accepts. Hence, she is the friend of all the great, benevolent, and charitable enterprises of the age, watches with attentive eye the developments of God's Providence, and is ever willing to fulfil her vocation in furtherance of the millennial glory, when the kingdoms of this world shall become the kingdoms of our Lord and his Christ, and Jesus shall reign king of nations, as he now does king of saints. These sublime and catholic principles are definitely laid down in her standards, namely in her—

I. *Liturgy,* portraying her mode of worship.

II. In her *Doctrinal Basis* laid down in the forms of Licensure and Ordination, contained in the Constitution for District Synods, viz., the *Bible* as the only infallible rule of faith and practice, and the *Augsburg Confession* so far as the fundamental doctrines of the Bible are concerned.

III. In the Formula of Government and Discipline for individual churches, for District Synods, and for the General Synod; and,

IV. In her Hymn-Book.

The *features* of the Churches of the General Synod, though liberal and open to improvement in non-essentials *are fixed, as also clearly defined, and adapted for Millennial Extension.*

APPENDIX, I.

New Plan for Christian Union.

The publication of the present writer, entitled *Fraternal Appeal to the American Churches, with a New Plan for Protestant Union on Apostolical Principles*, was first published in the American Biblical Repository, of Andover, in January and April, 1838, and subsequently several times as a separate volume, with numerous additions. For the satisfaction of those who have not seen this work, we will append the Circular Invitation published in 1845, after the book had been extensively circulated and generally approved. It was prepared and first printed by the present writer, then sent to each of the individuals whose name is attached to it, and subsequently published with all the names. Its object was to make a beginning in carrying out the plan proposed in the book. It is worthy of note, that in the history of the origin of the Evangelical Alliance, published in 1846, and appended to the minutes of the British Branch of it, this plan is referred to as having, next to the Scriptures, given the first impulse to the formation[1] of that noble institution of world-wide celebrity and usefulness.

Overture for Christian Union.

Submitted for the Consideration of the Evangelical Denominations in the United States.

Christian Brethren:

The undersigned respectfully address you, in the name of the Lord Jesus, on the great and cardinal interests of our common Christianity. That the blessed Saviour de-

[1] See Appendix, IV.

signed an intimate union between the different members of his mystical body, the Church, is elevated above all doubt by his own declaration, "One is your Master, Christ, and ye are all *brethren.*" That the preservation of this union possessed supreme importance in his view, he has himself taught us in his memorable prayer, "Neither pray I for these alone, but for them also who shall believe on me through their word; that they all may be *one*, as thou Father art in me and I in thee, that they also may be one in us, that the world may believe that thou hast sent me." The Church is represented by the great apostle as the "body of Christ;" and we are taught that "There is *one* body and one spirit, even as ye are called in one hope of your calling; *one* Lord, *one* faith, *one* baptism;" thus manifestly inculcating the spirit of unity in the Church, and representing the entire community of believers as substantially one body, into which all are admitted by the ordinance baptism, and in which they profess substantially the same faith and cherish the same hopes.

This language, it is conceded, does not specify the precise extent to which unity of visible organization shall be required. Nor is this fact determined elsewhere in Scripture, in the abstract. Yet does the metaphor of the apostle manifestly imply intimacy of relation; for, although there are, ordinarily, different members belonging to one body, they are always closely connected with each other. Yea, this connection is vital, is essential to their existence, and that member of the body becomes a putrid mass which is wholly severed from the living trunk.

Under these circumstances, it becomes a duty of surpassing importance to inquire, what are the nature and extent of the union so highly prized by the Saviour, and so vital to the prosperity of his body, the Church. If the New

Testament does not present a solution of this question *in theory*, the point is virtually solved by the practice of the Church under the guidance of the Saviour and his inspired apostles. This union, if we mistake not, consisted not in the subjection of the entire Church in any country under one supreme judicatory; much less in the subjugation of the whole visible Church on earth under one head or pope; neither did it consist in absolute unanimity of doctrinal views; for this did not exist even in the apostolic age; but, on the other hand, its features were:—

a. Unity of name. The whole body was styled the *Christian* Church, and its different parts were discriminated by the addition of geographical designations to the common name; such as, the church of Antioch, of Jerusalem, of Corinth. Sectarian names—that is, names based upon diversity of views or predilections, such as the church of Paul, or of Apollos, or Cephas, or Luther, or Calvin, or Wesley—were most unequivocally discountenanced.

b. Unity in fundamentals, whilst diversity in non-essentials was conceded, and the "brother who was weak in the faith was received, but not to doubtful disputation."

c. Mutual acknowledgment of each other's acts of discipline. Hence, "letters of commendation" (2 *Cor.* iii. 1–4)* were required of travelling brethren; and even the so-called Apostolic Canons provided that persons under discipline in the church of one place shall not be admitted to privileges in another.

d. Sacramental and ministerial intercommunion was a highly important and influential feature. "For we being many, are one bread, and *one body*, because we are all partakers of that one bread." The practice of sacramental

* By later writers termed literæ communicatoriæ, and *γραμματα κοινωνικα*.

communion extended indiscriminately to all whom they acknowledged as true disciples of Christ. "Forasmuch," said Peter, in vindication of his communion with men uncircumcised, "as God gave them the like gift as he did unto us who believed on the Lord Jesus Christ, what was I, that I could withstand God?" The existence of ministerial acknowledgment and communion is incontestably established by the Apostolic Canons and synodical decrees, enacted to guard against their abuse.

e. Convention of the different Churches of the land in synod or council, for the purpose of mutual consultation and ecclesiastical regulation. Of such a meeting we have an example in *Acts* xv.; and the earliest uninspired accounts extant of synodical meetings in the second century represent them as subserving the same ends.*

Thus was the great body of the primitive Church united into one fraternity by cords of love and mutual recognition; whilst those, and those only, were denied ecclesiastical communion who were excommunicated for immorality or denounced as fundamentally corrupt in the faith.

But how different the present condition of the Christian Church is, must be known to every intelligent friend of the Redeemer, and has been the subject of almost universal lamentation. Now she is cut up into sectarian branches, into divisions based on diversity of doctrinal views or forms of government, and not, as in the times of the Apostles, on contiguity of location. Different portions of the Church thus occupy the same geographical location, and in the absence of express mutual recognition and demonstration of substantial unity, alienation of affections, and conflicting interests of

* For the historical proofs of the above positions, we must refer to the Fraternal Appeal, or Plan of Christian Union, ed. 3d, New York, published by Taylor.

various kinds, pecuniary, literary, theological and sectarian, naturally arise, which prove wedges of discord to sever the body of Christ. And what enlightened friend of Zion must not confess, that it is the divided, the fractional, the isolated, and in some measure even the hostile condition of Protestantism, which has shorn the Church of so much of her strength? Who can doubt that these divisions tend to destroy community of interest and sympathy of feeling among the members of the Christian family? that they cast a sectarian veil over the mind in the study of the sacred volume, that they prejudice the ungodly world against Christianity itself, that they split up and fritter away the energies of the Protestant world, paralyzing her aggressive powers, and wasting, by want of concert, and often even in internal contention, those resources which ought to have been expended in converting the heathen and papal world?

The weakness of Protestantism undoubtedly lies in its divided and disjointed state; or, rather, in the principle on which its divisions are constructed. The faithful members of these departments of the Protestant Church are indeed actuated by proper motives, so far as the cultivation of their own hearts, and their labors for the conversion of others, are concerned; nor can the professed object of these associations themselves be repudiated, namely, the more successful advancement of truth and righteousness. But the very principle of the division habitually obtrudes sinister or at least secondary objects, so as virtually to postpone the claims of fundamental Christianity to those of separate sects; thus proving a grievous evil in Zion, preventing the necessary concentration of energies physical, intellectual, and moral, greatly impairing the moral influence of the Gospel, and impeding the formation of a correct Christian public sentiment throughout the world.

Happily, the attention of the Church has been extensively arrested by the deficiencies of the present Protestant organization. To say nothing of the efforts of eminent disciples of Christ in the last two centuries, leading minds of the present day, in our own and foreign lands, have had their attention fixed upon it. Not a few have spoken through the press, and there seems to be a prevailing impression that the time is at hand when something should be done in earnest to heal *the great schism*, to resist the encroachments of this Antichrist of the Protestant Churches. In our own country different associations have existed, and several public meetings have of late been held, attended by some of the most respectable divines of our country, for the promotion of Christian union; and the spirit of Christian union was increasingly manifest during the anniversaries of our national societies at New York, last spring. In Europe, the effort has been headed by such men as Rev. Dr. Merle D'Aubigne of Geneva, Rev. Monod of France, Rev. Kuntze of Prussia, Dr. Harris of England, Dr. Chalmers of Scotland. "I trust," said Dr. Chalmers, when introducing to the Assembly of the Free Church in Scotland his friends from the Continent, "you will not charge me with over-liberality if I say, as I do from my conscience, that among the great majority of Evangelical Dissenters in this country, I am not aware of any topics of difference which I do not regard as so many men of straw, and I shall be exceedingly glad if these gentlemen get the hearts of the various denominations to meet together and consent to make a bonfire of them." During the late session of that Assembly, a delightful meeting was held in Edinburgh for the promotion of Christian union, at which the practice of union was most happily exemplified, as was its theory forcibly established. At this meeting not less than eight different denominations were represented, viz.: the Reformed Church of France and Geneva, the Episcopal, the Free Church, the Secession Church, the Wesleyan Methodist, the Baptist, and the Independent Churches. A subsequent still larger meeting was held a few weeks since in Liverpool, in which persons of nineteen different denominations participated, and glorious progress for union was made.

In like manner, at the recent meeting of the General Synod of the Lutheran Church in the United States, convened in Philadelphia, the subject of Christian Union was discussed and acted on with great interest and deliberateness. Two plans were proposed: one by the Rev. Dr. Stockton of the Protestant Methodist Church, and one by Rev. Dr. Schmucker, the chairman of the General Synod's committee. Whilst some features of the former were regarded with much favor, the latter plan was adopted in full, as embodied in the following resolutions:—

Resolved, I. That a committee be appointed by this body, to be styled the "*Committee of Conference on Christian Union.*"

II. It shall be the duty of this committee to confer with similar committees appointed by other religious denominations, and with other prominent individuals of different denominations, on the great subject of Christian Union, and to report to the next General Synod such measures as may be agreed upon in such conference, to be recommended to the different religious denominations.

III. The design to be aimed at, by the measures thus to be recommended, is not to amalgamate the several denominations into one Church, nor to impair, in any degree, the independent control of each denomination over its own affairs and interests, but to present to the world a more formal profession and practical proof of our mutual recognition of each other as integral parts of the visible Church of Christ on earth, as well as of our fundamen al unity of faith, and readiness to co-operate harmoniously in the advancement of objects of common interest.

IV. That this committee shall consist of three ministers and two laymen, belonging to some synod or synods connected with the General Synod, and that they report to the next General Synod.

This committee, having consulted with the other subscribers, we unitedly submit to you an outline of that plan of union by which we hope the evils of schism can be gradually obviated, and the great and glorious object of Christian Union be eventually attained. We premise, that in the prosecution of this enterprise, the leadings of Providence should be observed and followed. Such steps and such only ought to be taken as the Church or judicatory, of whatever rank concerned, is prepared to adopt with considerable unanimity. Attempts which terminate in new divisions are obviously premature and unwise. And we may premise as fundamental principles, that the plan to be adopted must possess the following attributes: 1. It must require of no one the renunciation of any doctrine or opinion believed by him to be true, nor the profession of anything he regards as erroneous. The accession of any one denomination to this union, does not imply any sanction of the peculiarities of any other. 2. It must concede to each denomination the right to retain its own organization for government, discipline, and worship, or to alter it at option. 3. It must dissuade no one from discussing fundamentals and non-fundamentals, if done in the spirit of Christian love. 4. The plan must be such as is applicable to all *Evangelical, fundamentally Orthodox Churches*, and must not aim at inducing some of the denominations to relinquish their peculiar views, but must be based on the existing common ground of doctrine, and erect a superstructure of kindly feeling, and harmonious intercourse, and fraternal co-operation. 5. Each denomination may at option adopt any part, or all the proposed features of union.

With these preliminary specifications, we propose:

I. As one object of this union is to bear witness to the truth, and as well to impress upon ourselves as to exhibit to the world the fundamental doctrinal unity of the Evangelical Protestant Churches, therefore, *any denomination wishing to accede to this Union, can do so by a resolution of its highest judicatory, embodying its assent to the common ground of Christian doctrine, as exhibited, for the present, in the appended selection from the articles of the principal Protestant Confessions.* The most respectable writers on Christian union, and ecclesiastical bodies also, so far as they have expressed themselves, have, with few exceptions, agreed that the vital principle of Protestantism lies not in the peculiarities of any sect, but in the points adopted by them all; and that the requisition of doctrinal agreement shall be confined to this common ground of Protestant doctrine, to the doctrines and aspects of doctrine in which they are known to agree. This may be adopted as the expressed sentiment of the principal friends of union. A preliminary attempt has therefore been made to express this common ground of doctrine, in the very language of the different Protestant confessions. This expose of doctrine, let it be remembered, is not an original or new creed, but a selection of articles or parts of articles from the principal existing Protestant creeds, every part of which has already been sanctioned by one or other of the respective denominations. Not a single original sentence is contained in it. If any acknowledged orthodox denomination should still find in it a sentiment to which it objects, the clause expressing it may be excepted in the vote of adoption, and it will thereafter be omitted by all; for the design of this expose is, that it shall contain only the doctrines received by all the so-called Evangelical Orthodox Churches. It has, however, already been examined and approved by some of the most distinguished divines of our country, belonging to nine different denominations, and therefore probably contains no sentiment inconsistent with the received doctrines of any so-called Orthodox Protestant Church. This expose — which, as it contains the so-called Apostles' Creed, and a fundamental digest of the principal Protestant creeds, may be styled the United Apostolic Protestant Confession — is here presented only in a preliminary way, as one of the means to bring about a general convention of delegates from the different Protestant denominations of our land, and perhaps of other lands; and at such meeting it can be amended, or an entirely original one be adopted in its place. Yet, as it really is the joint production and the joint property of the different denominations, it will not only bear on its face the evidence of union, but also be more welcome and be more cordially received; for each will feel that it has contributed something to this common symbolic stock. It would, moreover, be pleasant, as the several creeds promoted separation, to turn them now into an instrument of union. A creed on this principle of eclecticism, can certainly be formed satisfactory to all; but it will be far more difficult to frame an original one equally acceptable. Such an eclectic creed will, moreover, form a *historico-symbolic union* and connection between the Church in the Apostolic age, in the age of the Reformation, and in our own day,— a fact of no small importance in historical Christianity.

Each denomination will, however, retain its present creed, and other directories for the reception and discipline of ministers and members, and may alter or amend them at option as heretofore.

As the features of this plan do not necessarily interfere with other denominational standards of government and discipline, inferior judicatories of every grade, and even individual congregations, can discuss its claims, and, if approved, vote their assent to its features, and adopt it for themselves as far as it does not interfere with their existing engagements. Thus any conference, presbytery, classis, synod, and convention can adopt the plan by voting their assent to the proposed United Apostolic Protestant Confession, and resolving to practise such of the additional features as they may judge suitable to their case, and to bring the subject before their highest judicatories. Inferior judicatories might also appoint a delegate to a contiguous co-ordinate judicatory of one or more sister churches. Individual congregations might, in addition to assenting to the expose of Protestant doctrine, resolve to unite with sister churches in voluntary associations for the advancement of the Bible, Tract, Sabbath School cause. An annual or semi-annual Union meeting of the different congregational Sabbath Schools of a town, or village, or ward of a city, to hear a sermon on some aspect of the cause, and for other exercises, would doubtless cultivate the spirit of brotherly love, especially among the rising generation. In short, although the plan contemplates ultimately the unity of spirit and fraternal co-operation of entire congregations, the effort must begin in every church with individuals, and often find its way up through the inferior judicatories to those of the higher and the highest order.

II. Let the Supreme judicatories of the several orthodox churches resolve to open and sustain a regular ecclesiastical intercourse, by sending a delegate to the stated meetings of the highest judicatory of each such denomination, who ought to be received as advisory members, but have no vote. This practice which already exists between some Protestant denominations has been attended by the happiest effects, and ought to be extended as far as convenient to all.

III. Co-operation of the different associated churches in voluntary associations, local and general, should be encouraged, as far as the sentiment of the respective denominations is prepared for it, under constitutions, avowing the United Apostolic Protestant Confession, and securing equal rights to all its members. This principle is especially applicable to Bible, Tract, Sabbath School, and foreign Missionary Societies, and has already been introduced in a large portion of the Protestant denominations.

IV. The Bible should, as much as possible, be made the text-book in all theological, congregational, and Sabbath School instruction.

V. One general Anniversary Celebration should be held at some central place, under the management of a committee of arrangements, one member of which is to be selected from each confederated denomination, and after its formal accession to the union, to be appointed by its supreme judicatory. State and smaller union celebrations might also be held, and occasionally, though not statedly, a universal or œcumenical Protestant convention, like that proposed to be held in London in 1846.

VI. Free sacramental communion ought to be occasionally practised by all whose views of duty allow it.

VII. The formal adoption of these features, or of any part of them, if the first be included, shall constitute the adopting body an integral part of the Apostolic Protestant Union. Should any denomination wish to reserve any one of the features, except the first, for future consideration, such reservation shall not invalidate its accession to the residue.

But in the name of the bleeding Church, let us go forward in this glorious work. The first and greatest advocate of Christian union, the Saviour himself, will go before us, and light will shine on our path as we advance. We shall see, from step to step, what his providence directs. Nor can we doubt, that, whether our object is accomplished in our way or not, the effort will redound to the glory of God. If it be found, that we are not yet prepared to walk together, even in the things in which we are agreed, the Master may throw us into the furnace of affliction, to melt away our asperities. But amid all circumstances of encouragement or depression, let our motto be: "*Look upward, and press onward*," in reliance on the blessing of Him who said, "Lo, I am with you alway, even unto the end of the world."

N. B. The present plan is presented for the preliminary consideration of the churches, and it is proposed to hold a meeting during the Anniversaries in May next* in New York, preparatory to final action, at which all those favorable to the general

---

* Soon after the issuing of this circular, the notice for the meeting of the Evangelical Alliance in London, during the succeeding August of 1846, was announced, in consequence of which this meeting was indefinitely postponed, for two reasons: first, because many of the most active friends of our American enterprise expected to be absent in Europe, and secondly, it was also deemed proper for us to await the results of the more extended meeting in London, which embraced the whole civilized world. On our return from England, it was believed by the delegates to the Evangelical Alliance, that an American branch of that noble institution would virtually accomplish the same end in the premises. But when an attempt was made to organize such an American branch, the parties differed as to the admission of slaveholders, and could not arrive at any satisfactory result. Soon afterwards the political discussions of slavery ensued, and hitherto nothing of a general nature has been done, although the churches are again pondering the subject.

object are invited to attend. Further notice will be given. The major part of the subscribers expect to be present.

S. S. Schmucker, D. D., Prof. of Theol., Theol. Seminary, Gettysburg, Pa.
C. P. Krauth, D. D., Pres. Penn. College, Gettysburg, Pa.
G. B. Miller, D. D., Prof. Theol., Theol. Sem., Hartwick, N. Y.
Hon. Wm. C. Bouck, Fultonham, New York.
C. A. Morris, Esq., York, Penn.
Com. on Christian Union of the General Synod of Lutheran Church in United States.

Rev. J. Hawes, D. D., Past. Congreg. Church, Hartford, Conn.
Rev. L. Bacon, D. D., Past. Congreg. Church, New Haven, Conn.
Rev. Wm. Hill, D. D., Past. Presb. Church, Winchester, Pa.
Rev. L. Mayer, D. D., late Prof. of Theol. in Theol. Sem., Mercersburg, Pa.
Rev. G. Spring, D. D., Pastor of Presb. Church, New York.
Rev. G. W. Bethune, D. D., Past. Reformed Dutch Ch., Phila.
Rev. R. Emory, Pres't Dickinson College, Carlisle, Pa.
Rev. J. P. Durbin, D. D., Past. of M. E. Ch., and late Prof. of Dickinson College.
Rev. C. A. Goodrich, D. D., Prof. in Theol. Sem., N. H., Conn.
Rev. R. Baird, D. D., Sec'y Amer. Evangelical Society, N. Y.
Rev. E. L. Hazelius, D. D., Prof. Theol., Theol. Sem., Lexington, S. C.
Rev. B. P. Aydelott, D. D., of the Prot. Episcopal Church, Pres't of Woodward College, Cincinnati.
Rev. G. B. Cheever, D. D., Editor of N. Y. Evangelist.
Rev. P. Church, D. D., Past. Baptist Church, Rochester, N. Y.
Rev. T. H. Cox, D. D., Past. Presb. Church, Brooklyn, N. Y.
Rev. D. McConaughy, Pres't Wash. College, Washington, Pa.
Rev. E. Pond, D. D., Prof. of Theol., Theol. Sem., Bangor.
Rev. Wm. Patton, D. D., Pastor Presb. Church, New York.
Rev. B. Kurtz, D. D., Editor Lutheran Observer, Baltimore.
Rev. A. Converse, Editor of Christian Observer, Philada.
Rev. J. Parker, D. D., Pastor of Presb. Church, Philada.
Rev. J. G. Morris, D. D., Pastor of Lutheran Church, Baltimore.
Rev. J. E. Welsh, of Baptist Church, Burlington, N. J.
Rev. H. P. Tappan, D. D., Prof. University of New York.
Rev. J. F. Berg, D. D., German Reformed Church, Editor Protestant Quarterly Review, Phila.
Rev. F. Waters, D. D., Protestant Methodist Church, Baltimore.
Alex. Henry, Esq., Presbyterian Church, Philadelphia.
Rev. E. Heiner, Pastor German Ref. Church, Baltimore.

Rev. G. W. Musgrave, D. D.., Pastor Presb. Ch., Baltimore.
Rev. B. C. Wolf, D. D., Pastor German Ref. Church, Baltimore.
Rev. B. M. Smith, Pastor Presb. Church, Staunton, Va.
Rev. R. W. Bailey, Presbyterian Church, Staunton, Va.
Rev. C. G. Weyl, Editor Lutheran Hirtenstimme, Baltimore.
Rev. W. R. De Witt, D. D., Pastor Presb. Church, Harrisb'g, Pa.
Rev. W. Hamilton, Methodist Episcopal Church, Baltimore.
Rev. J. C. Watson, Pastor of Presb. Church, Gettysburg, Pa.
Rev. J. Collins, Pastor of Methodist Epis. Church, Baltimore.

P. S. An official communication has just been received, addressed to the subscriber, as chairman of the Lutheran General Synod's Committee on Union, from the following gentlemen, as Committee of the Cumberland Presbyterian General Assembly for Christian Union: —

S. S. Schmucker.

Rev. M. Bird, Cumberland Presb. Church, Uniontown, Pa.
Rev. A. M. Bryan, Cumberland Presb. Church, Pittsburg, Pa.
Alex. Miller, Esq., Cumberland Presb. Church, Pittsburg, Pa.

PART I. The Apostles' Creed.

"I believe in God the Father Almighty, the Maker of heaven and earth: And in Jesus Christ, his only Son, our Lord; who was conceived by the Holy Ghost, born of the virgin Mary, suffered under Pontius Pilate, was crucified, dead and buried. The third day he rose from the dead, he ascended into heaven, and sitteth on the right hand of God the Father Almighty, from thence he shall come to judge the quick and the dead.

"I believe in the Holy Ghost, the holy catholic or universal church; the communion of saints; the forgiveness of sins; the resurrection of the body, and the life everlasting."

PART II. The United Protestant Confession.

Art. I. *Of the Scriptures.*

The Holy Scripture containeth all things necessary to

salvation: so that whatsoever is not read therein, nor may be proved thereby, is not to be required of any man, that it should be believed as an article of the faith, or be thought requisite or necessary to salvation.* Under the name of the Holy Scriptures, or the Word of God written, are now contained all the books of the Old and New Testament, which are these: Genesis, Exodus, Leviticus, Numbers, Deuteronomy, Joshua, Judges, Ruth, I. Samuel, II. Samuel, I. Kings, II. Kings, I. Chronicles, II. Chronicles, Ezra, Nehemiah, Esther, Job, Psalms, Proverbs, Ecclesiastes, Song of Solomon, Isaiah, Jeremiah, Lamentations, Ezekiel, Daniel, Hosea, Joel, Amos, Obadiah, Jonah, Micah, Nahum, Habakkuk, Zephaniah, Haggai, Zechariah, Malachi, Matthew, Mark, Luke, John, Acts of the Apostles, Epistle to the Romans, I. Corinthians, II. Corinthians, Galatians, Ephesians, Philippians, Colossians, I. Thessalonians, II. Thessalonians, I. Timothy, II. Timothy, Titus, Philemon, Hebrews, Epistle of James, I. Peter, II. Peter, I. John, II. John, III. John, Jude, Revelation.

All which are given by inspiration of God to be the rule of faith and life. The books commonly called Apocrypha, not being of divine inspiration, are no part of the canon of Scripture.[1]

ART. II. *Of God and the Trinity.*

Our churches, with one accord, teach that there is one God, eternal, incorporeal, indivisible, infinite in power, wis-

* Articles of the Episcopal Church, Art. VI., and of the Discipline of the Methodist Church, Art. V.

[1] Ratio Disciplinæ, or Constitution of the Congregational Churches, Art. I. §§ 2, 3. Confession of the Presbyterian Church, Art. I. §§ 2, 3. Confession of the Baptist Churches, (adopted in 1742,) Chap. I. §§ 2, 3. The Confession of the Dutch Reformed Church is also of the same general doctrinal import.

dom, and goodness, the Creator and Preserver of all things visible and invisible, who governs the same by his eternal counsel and providence,[2] and yet that there are three persons, the Father, the Son, and the Holy Spirit.[3]

ART. III. *Of the Son of God and the Atonement.*

They likewise teach, that the Word, that is, the Son of God, assumed human nature, so that the two natures, human and divine, united in one person, constitute one Christ, who is true God and man; born of the virgin Mary; and truly suffered, was crucified, died, and was buried, that he might be a sacrifice for the sins of men.[4]

ART. IV. *Of Human Depravity.*

God having made a covenant of works, and of life thereupon, with our first parents, they, seduced by the subtilty and temptation of Satan, did wilfully transgress and break the covenant by eating the forbidden fruit.[5] By this sin they fell from their original righteousness and communion with God, and so became dead in sin.[6] They being the root of all mankind, a corrupted nature is conveyed to all their posterity descending from them by ordinary generation.[7] The condition of man, after the fall of Adam, is such,[8] that his will is neither forced, nor by any absolute necessity of nature determined to do good or evil;[9] but it does not pos-

[2] German Reformed, Heidelberg, C. Q. 26.
[3] Lutheran and Moravian (United Brethren's) Confession, Art. I.
[4] Idem, Art. III.
[5] Congregational, Art VI. 1.
[6] Presbyterian, Art. VI. 2.
[7] Congregational, Art VI. 3. Baptist, Chapter VI. § 3.
[8] Episcopal, Art. X.
[9] Baptist, Presbyterian, and Congregational, IX. 1.

sess the power, without the influence of the Holy Spirit, of being just before God, or yielding spiritual obedience; but this is accomplished in the heart, when the Holy Spirit is received through the word.[10]

ART. V. *Of Justification.*

We are accounted righteous before God only for the merit of our Lord and Saviour Jesus Christ by faith; and not for our own works or deservings.[11] This faith must bring forth good fruits; and it is our duty to perform those good works which God has commanded, because he has enjoined them, and not in the expectation of thereby meriting justification before him.[12] Good works cannot put away our sins, and endure the severity of God's judgment.[13]

ART. VI. *Of the Church.*

The visible Church, which is called catholic or universal under the Gospel, (not confined to one nation,) consists of all those throughout the world that profess the true religion, and is the kingdom of the Lord Jesus Christ. Unto this catholic, visible church, Christ hath given the ministry, oracles, and ordinances of God.[14] For the true unity of the Church, it is not necessary that the same rites and ceremonies, instituted by men, should be everywhere observed.[15] The purest churches under heaven are subject both to mixture and error;[16] nevertheless, Christ always hath had, and

[10] Lutheran and Moravian Conf., Art. XVIII.
[11] Episcopal Conf., Art XI., and Methodist, Art. IX.
[12] Lutheran and Moravian Conf., Art. VI.
[13] Methodist Discip., Art. X., and Episcopal Conf. Art. XII.
[14] Presbyterian Conf., Art. XXV., 2, 3.
[15] Lutheran and Moravian, Art. VII.
[16] Presb. XXV. 3, and Cong. XXVI. 3, Baptist, Chap. XXVII. § 3.

ever will have, a visible kingdom in this world to the end thereof, of such as believe in him, and make profession of his name.[17] There is no other head of the Church but the Lord Jesus Christ, nor can the Pope of Rome in any sense be the head thereof.[18]

ART. VII. *Of the Sacraments, Baptism, and the Lord's Supper.*

The sacraments were instituted, not only as marks of a Christian profession among men, but rather as signs and evidences of the divine disposition towards us, tendered for the purpose of exciting and confirming the faith of those who use them.[19] There be only two sacraments ordained by Christ our Lord in the Gospel, that is to say, Baptism and the Supper of the Lord.[20] Baptism is ordained not only for the solemn admission of the party baptized into the visible church, but also to be unto him a sign of the covenant of grace, of regeneration, of remission of sins,[21] and of his giving up unto God through Jesus Christ, to walk in the newness of life.[22] The Supper of the Lord is not only a sign of the love that Christians ought to have among themselves, but rather is a sacrament of our redemption by Christ's death.[23]

In this sacrament Christ is not offered up, nor any sacrifice made at all for remission of sins of the quick or dead; so that the popish sacrifice of the mass, as they call it, is

[17] Congregational Conf., Art. XXVI., 3. Baptist, Chap. XXVII. § 3.
[18] Congregational, XXVI. 4, and Presbyterian, XXV. 6.
[19] Lutheran and Moravian Conf., Art. XIII.
[20] Presb., Art. XXVII., 4, and Cong., XXVIII., 4.
[21] Presb., Art. XXVIII., 1.
[22] Baptist, Chap. XXX., § 1. Presb., Art. XXVIII., § 1. Cong., Art. XXIX., § 1.
[23] Methodist Disc., Art. XVIII., and Episc., Art. XXVIII.

most injurious to Christ's one only sacrifice.[24] That do.trine which maintains a change of the bread and wine into Christ's body and blood, (commonly called transubstantiation,) by consecration of a priest, or in any other way, is repugnant not to Scripture alone, but even to common sense and reason.[25] The denying of the cup to the people, and worshipping the elements, or carrying them about for adoration, are all contrary to the institution of Christ.[26]

Art. VIII. *Of Purgatory, etc.*

The Romish doctrine concerning purgatory, worshiping as well of images as of relics, and also invocation of saints, is repugnant to the Word of God.[27]

Art. IX. *Liberty of Conscience.*

God alone is the Lord of conscience, and hath left it free from the doctrines and commandments of men, which are in any wise contrary to his Word, or beside it in matters of faith and worship. So that to believe such doctrines, or to obey such commandments out of conscience, is to betray true liberty of conscience; and the requiring of an implicit faith, and an absolute and blind obedience, is to destroy liberty of conscience and reason also.[28]

Art. X. *Of Civil Government.*

God, the Supreme Lord and King of all the world, hath

[24] Presb., Art. xxxix., 2, and Cong., xxx. 2. Baptist Chap. xxxii., § 2.
[25] Baptist, Ch. xxxii., § 6. Presb. Conf., Art. xxxix. 6, and Cong. xxx. 6.
[26] Presb., xxix. 4, Cong., xxx. 4. Baptist, Chap. xxxiii. § 4.
[27] Methodist Disc., Art xiv., and Episcopal, Art. xxii.
[28] Presb. xx. 2. Baptist, xxi., § 2.

ordained civil magistrates to be under him, over the people, for his own glory and the public good, and to this end hath armed them with power for the defence and encouragement of them that do good, and for the punishment of evil doers.[29] The power of the civil magistrate extendeth to all men, as well clergy as laity in things temporal, but hath no authority in things purely spiritual.[30] Christians ought to yield obedience to the civil officers and laws of the land, unless they should command something sinful, in which case it is a duty to obey God rather than man.[31]

ART. XI. *Communion of Saints.*

Saints are bound to maintain an holy fellowship and communion in the worship of God, and in performing such other spiritual services as tend to their mutual edification: As also in relieving each other in outward things, according to their several abilities and necessities; which communion, as God offereth opportunity, is to be extended to all those who, in every place, call upon the name of the Lord Jesus.[32]

ART. XII. *Of the Future Judgment and Retribution.*

At the end of the world Christ will appear for judgment; he will raise the dead; he will give to the pious eternal life and endless joys; but will condemn wicked men and devils to be punished without end.[33] As Christ would have us to be certainly persuaded that there shall be a day of judgment, to deter all men from sin, so will he have that day unknown to men, that they may shake off all carnal security, and be

[29] Cong., XXIV., 1, and Presb., XXXIII., 1. Baptist, XXV., § 1.
[30] Episc. XXXVII.
[31] Lutheran and Moravian, Art. XVI.
[32] Cong. XXVII. 2, and Presb. XXVI. 2. Baptist, Ch. XXVIII, § 1.
[33] Lutheran and Moravian, Conf., Art. XVII.

always watchful, because they know not at what hour the Lord will come, and may ever be prepared to say, *Come, Lord Jesus, come quickly. Amen.*[34]

APPENDIX, II.

Testimonials.

THE following are a few of the numerous testimonials sent to the author, soon after the publication of his work containing his *Plan for Protestant Union on Apostolical Principles.*

To Rev. Dr. Schmucker, from the Professors of the Theological Seminary at Andover.

The undersigned have paid some attention to the volume of Dr. Schmucker, entitled an "Appeal to the American Churches, with a Plan of Union on Apostolic Principles." Without expressing any opinion on the practicability of the precise plan of union recommended by Dr. Schmucker, we very cheerfully express our approbation of the general principles which he advocates in his Appeal, and our conviction that the whole subject which he discusses is worthy of the serious and devout attention of evangelical Christians. We cannot but hope that the extensive circulation and perusal of a volume imbued with so catholic and conciliatory a spirit as this, will be peculiarly useful at the present

[34] Baptist, Ch. XXXIV., § 3. Presbyterian, XXXIII. 3. Congregational, XXXII. 3.

day; that it will tend to enlarge and liberalize the hearts of good men, and induce them to think more of the great essential doctrines on which they agree, and less of the unessential points on which they may differ.

JUSTIN EDWARDS, D. D.,
Pres. of Andover Theol. Sem.
LEONARD WOODS, D. D.,
Abbot Prof. of Christ. Theol.
MOSES STUART,
Associate Prof. of Sacred Lit.
RALPH EMERSON, D. D.,
Brown Prof. of Eccl. Hist.
B. B. EDWARDS,
Prof. of Heb. Lang. and Lit.
EDWARDS A. PARK,
Bartlet Prof. of Sac. Rhetoric.

To Rev. Dr. Schmucker, from Prominent Lutheran Divines.

The plan of union proposed by the Rev. Dr. Schmucker, which was first communicated to the public through the pages of the Biblical Repository, has been attentively considered by me, and I do not hesitate to say, after a careful examination of its principles, that it accords, in my judgment, with the genius of our holy religion, as taught in the pages of the New Testament. I agree with him in the opinion that union is practicable, that it ought to take place, and that the accomplishment of it should be the sincere aim of all who love the Saviour, in our different religious denominations: because it will remove many heavy evils under which the Church now labors, facilitate the diffusion of religion, and arm the Church with power which will render it speedily triumphant to the ends of the earth. The union advocated is apostolical, such as existed in the days of the heralds of the gospel, and which, as much as anything else, imparted power to the preached word. Union then was strength, and now, if restored, would render our faith irresistible. I can scarcely persuade myself that he has imbibed the spirit of Jesus Christ in any considerable extent, who does not consider it a consummation most devoutly to be desired and sincerely prayed for. The final prayers of the Saviour on earth had reference to this blessed union,—"Neither pray I for them alone, but for them also which shall believe on me through their word: that they may be all one; as thou, Father, art in me, and I in thee, that they also may be one in us: that the world may believe that thou hast sent me."

The plan of Dr. Schmucker meets my approbation more fully than any other that has come to my knowledge, because it does not restrict itself to arguments for union, and eloquent declamation on the beauties of a harmonizing Church, whilst the way of bringing it about was left untouched. He has answered the question in a manner highly creditable to him as a theologian and a Christian. How is this to be effected? The mode of accomplishing it is intelligible, and by no means complicated; it secures all vital truth, guards against extensive innovation in existing institutions, does not run counter to that attachment to the formularies of government and discipline in any church to which we may belong, which is so natural, and places the united Church on a better basis to maintain internal peace, and to avoid dangerous dissensions, than has ever yet existed.

With these views, I anxiously wish that the Church of Jesus Christ in this country would take into most serious consideration the appeal which has been addressed to them on this subject. May the day not be distant when our eyes shall behold a convention of Christian divines deliberating in the spirit of the Master on this great subject, and b.inging forth their solemn decision in favor of union between Christian denominations, and of concentrated action in the great objects of the Christian enterprise!

C. P. KRAUTH, D. D.,
President of Pennsylvania College, Gettysburg.

GETTYSBURG, Dec. 17, 1838.

We, the undersigned, coincide in the above opinion of Dr. Krauth.

REV. ERNEST L. HAZELIUS, D. D.,
Principal of Theol. Sem., Lexington, S. C.
REV. GEO. B. MILLER, D. D.,
Principal of Hartwick Seminary, N. Y.
J. G. SCHMUCKER, D. D.,
Late Pastor of Lutheran Church, York, Pa.
LEVI STERNBERG, A. M.,
Assistant Professor in Hartwick Seminary, Cooperstown, N. Y.
BENJ. KELLER,
President of the Evan. Lutheran Synod of West Pennsylvania.
AUGUSTUS LOCHMAN, A. M.,
Pastor of the First Lutheran Church, York, Pa.
WM. M. REYNOLDS, A. M.,
Professor of the Latin Language and Literature, Penna. College.
HENRY I. SMITH,
Prof. of French and German Lang. and Lit. in Penna. College.

To the Rev. Dr. Schmucker.

DEAR SIR:—We have read with interested attention your "Appeal to the American Churches," in behalf of "Christian Union," and take pleasure in expressing our cordial assent to the scriptural arguments which it adduces, and our earnest wishes for the momentous object which it is designed to promote. We do not believe that there is a minister of our own denomination in the land, who would not hail with thankfulness the accomplishment of that object on just and truly catholic principles. The settlement of such principles forms the chief difficulty. We shall rejoice to see this removed, and Christians of every name united in affection, and acting in concert.

Although we cannot pledge ourselves to the adoption of a new creed, or the prosecution of any plan not of the most general and scriptural character, we think that the publication of your very able essay will be useful in presenting the whole subject to the notice of our countrymen, and diffusing much light on some of the points involved in it.

We are, very respectfully,

Your friends and brethren,

PHILIP F. MAYER, D. D.,
Pastor of St. John's Church, Phila.

CHAS. R. DEMME, D. D.,
President of the Evangelical Lutheran "Synod of Pennsylvania," and Pastor of Zion's and St. Michael's Church.

STEPHEN A. MEALY,
Pastor of St. Matthew's Church.

G. A REICHART,
Associate Pastor of Zion's and St. Michael's Church, Phila.

APPENDIX, III.

[To p. 98.]

To George Washington, President of the United States.

SIR: On this day, which becomes important in the annals of America, as marking the close of a splendid public life, devoted for near half a century to the service of your country, we the undersigned clergy of different denominations, residing in and near the City of Philadelphia, beg leave to join the v)ice of our fellow-citizens, in expressing a deep sense of your public services, in every department of trust and authority committed to you. But in our especial character as ministers of the gospel of Christ, we are more immediately bound to acknowledge the countenance which you have uniformly given to his holy religion.

In your public character we have uniformly beheld the edifying example of a civil ruler always acknowledging the superintendence of Divine Providence in the affairs of men; and confirming that example by the powerful recommendation of religion and morality, as the firmest basis of social happiness; more especially, in the following language of your affectionate parting address to your fellow-citizens: "Of all the dispositions and habits which lead to political prosperity, religion and morality are indispensable supports. In vain would that man claim the tribute of patriotism, who should labor to subvert these great pillars of social happiness, the surest props of the duties of men and citizens. The mere politician, equally with the religious man, ought to respect and cherish them. A volume could not trace all their connections with private and public felicity. Let us with caution indulge the supposition that morality can be maintained without religion. Reason and experience forbid us to expect that national morality can prevail in exclusion of religious principles." Should the importance of these just and pious sentiments be duly appreciated and regarded, we confidently trust that the prayers you have offered for the prosperity of our common country will be answered. In these prayers we most fervently unite; and with equal fervor we join in those which the numerous public bodies, that represent the citizens of these States, are offering for their beloved Chief. We most devoutly implore the divine blessing to attend you in your retirement, to make it in all respects comfortable to you, to satisfy you with length of days, and finally to receive you into happiness and glory, infinitely greater than this world can bestow.

Wm. White,
Ashbel Green,
Wm. Smith,
John Ewing,
Samuel Jones,
Wm. Hendel,
Samuel Magaw,
Henry Helmuth,
Samuel Blair,
Nicholas Collin,
Robt, Annan,
Wm. Marshall,
John Meder,
John Andrews,
J. F. Schmidt,
Robt. Blackwell,
Wm. Rogers,
Thos. Ustick,
Andrew Hunter,
John Dickins,
J. Jones,
Joseph Turner,
Ezekiel Cooper,
Morgan J. Rhees,
James Abercrombie.

APPENDIX, IV.

[To p. 242.]

On the Origin of the Evangelical Alliance.

In order the more to commend the foregoing *Plan for Christian Union* to the serious attention of enlightened friends of Zion in America, the following statement of its happy influence in Great Britain is appended. At the meeting of the Evangelical Alliance in London, in 1846, a pamphlet was distributed among the members, entitled "*Historical Sketch of the Evangelical Alliance.*" It had been prepared by the Rev. Dr. King of Glasgow, at the request of the Provisional Committee of a preliminary meeting, and unanimously adopted as a correct narrative of the origin and preliminary steps for the formation of the great Evangelical Alliance at London, which embraced about a thousand of the most distinguished Christians of all the principal denominations in the Protestant world. It has since held meetings in Germany, Holland, France, &c., and exerted a powerful influence in favor of religious liberty, true piety, and Christian Union. The pamphlet had been printed in advance of this meeting, and was distributed among its members. After having mentioned the frequent injunctions of God's word to Union among the followers of the Saviour, and the progress of infidelity and popery as calling for greater activity among Christians, that history proceeds as follows:

"On the other hand, the leadings of Providence presented uncommon facilities for Christian union. The asperities of party which, in former ages, had obscured and almost concealed the catholicity of the church, had become softened and diminished. The principle of toleration which had once no open friend, had no more a declared foe; and this single change strongly indicated a great revolution of sentiment. Religious and benevolent societies, embracing Christians of different denominations, maintained their ground and increased in strength, showing the stability of the foundation on which they were reared. Interesting movements had taken place expressly for the promotion of brotherhood, and the diffusion of its blessings. To notice a few examples, and to begin with the *remotest*—much praise is due to Dr. Schmucker of America, for his zealous endeavors to associate Christians of different denominations across the Atlantic, and to concentrate their efforts on objects of common interest. Whatever may be thought of his scheme of union, all Christians must admire the spirit by which it was dictated, and rejoice in *the practical good of which the proposal and discussion of it have been confessedly productive.*"

INDEX.

www.ingramcontent.com/pod-product-compliance
Lightning Source LLC
LaVergne TN
LVHW010227110826
845151LV00004B/1211

9781425526504